D1090288

ASHE Higher Education Report: Volume 34, Nu
Kelly Ward, Lisa E. Wolf-Wendel, Series Editors

Theoretical Perspectives on Student Success: Understanding the Contributions of the Disciplines

Laura W. Perna
Scott L. Thomas

Theoretical Perspectives on Student Success: Understanding the
Contributions of the Disciplines
Laura W. Perna and Scott L. Thomas
ASHE Higher Education Report: Volume 34, Number 1
Kelly Ward, Lisa E. Wolf-Wendel, Series Editors

ISSN 1551-6970   electronic ISSN 1554-6306   ISBN 978-0-4704-1078-3

The ASHE Higher Education Report is part of the Jossey-Bass Higher and Adult
Education Series and is published six times a year by Wiley Subscription Services,
Inc., A Wiley Company, at Jossey-Bass, 989 Market Street, San Francisco,
California 94103-1741.

For subscription information, see the Back Issue/Subscription Order Form
in the back of this volume.

CALL FOR PROPOSALS: Prospective authors are strongly encouraged to contact
Kelly Ward (kaward@wsu.edu) or Lisa Wolf-Wendel (lwolf@ku.edu). See "About
the ASHE Higher Education Report Series" in the back of this volume.

Visit the Jossey-Bass Web site at **www.josseybass.com.**

Printed in the United States of America on acid-free recycled paper.

The ASHE Higher Education Report is indexed in CIJE: Current Index to Jour-
nals in Education (ERIC), Current Abstracts (EBSCO), Education Index/Abstracts
(H.W. Wilson), ERIC Database (Education Resources Information Center),
Higher Education Abstracts (Claremont Graduate University), IBR & IBZ: Inter-
national Bibliographies of Periodical Literature (K.G. Saur), and Resources in
Education (ERIC).

Advisory Board

The ASHE Higher Education Report Series is sponsored by the Association for the Study of Higher Education (ASHE), which provides an editorial advisory board of ASHE members.

Contents

Executive Summary

Federal, state, and local policymakers, K-12 and college administrators, and numerous researchers have invested substantial effort into improving and reducing gaps in student success. But our understanding of student success is limited, at least in part, by the wide array of theoretical and methodological approaches that characterize these efforts.

Drawing on a review of research published in four disciplines, this monograph proposes a conceptual model that policymakers, practitioners, and researchers may use to guide the development, implementation, and evaluation of policies and practices for improving success for all students and reducing persisting gaps in student success. The framework does not provide a model for understanding any specific student success outcome or stage but is designed to bring order to the wide array of theoretical and methodological approaches that, only when considered together, provide a comprehensive understanding of the ways that policymakers and practitioners may more usefully intervene to effectively promote student success.

After defining student success and explaining our procedures, the monograph describes the results of a multidisciplinary examination of the theoretical and methodological approaches that researchers have used to inform knowledge and understanding across a range of student success outcomes. The monograph then presents and describes the proposed conceptual model that ties this work together. We conclude by suggesting implications of the model for policy and practice and areas for further research.

A Conceptual Model for Understanding Disciplinary Approaches to Student Success

Our approach to developing the conceptual framework assumes the centrality of disciplinary perspectives for understanding student success. Disciplines bring specific methods for identifying, conceptualizing, and analyzing questions of student success. In every discipline, research design, data collection, and analysis reflect a researcher's response to a number of underlying philosophical questions that define what might be seen and what might be ignored in the inquiry. These epistemological elements are fundamentally related to disciplinary identities themselves.

To produce this monograph, we reviewed literature that examined ten indicators of student success in each of four selected disciplines: economics, sociology, psychology, and education. The ten indicators of student success that we considered are educational aspirations, academic preparation for college, college access, college choice, academic preparation in college, transfer among colleges, persistence to degree or program completion, postbaccalaureate enrollment, earnings, and educational attainment. With the goal of capitalizing on what scholars in these disciplines agree to be the best existing research on the components of student success, we limited the review to articles published between January 1, 1995, and June 30, 2005, in top journals in each of the four disciplines.

We drew six conclusions about disciplinary approaches to student success from our review: (1) theoretical approaches to understanding student success vary across disciplines; (2) the relative attention to student success in articles published in top journals varies across disciplines; (3) even within disciplines, aspects of student success that were examined vary; (4) methodological approaches and sources of data for exploring student success vary across disciplines and, as one might expect, are rather tightly bound to the theoretical stance employed; (5) the unit of analysis varies by disciplinary and theoretical approach; and (6) attention to differences in student success across groups varies across the four disciplines.

Building on the central conclusions of our disciplinary review, we propose a multilayered conceptual model for understanding student success. The four layers of the model are the internal context; the family context; the school context; and the broader social, economic, and political context. The proposed conceptual model has six underlying assumptions: (1) the relative contribution of different disciplinary and area perspectives to student success varies; (2) when considered together, multiple theoretical approaches yield more comprehensive understandings of student success; (3) student success is shaped by multiple levels of context; (4) student success processes vary across groups; (5) multiple methodological approaches contribute to knowledge of student success; and (6) student success is a longitudinal process.

Disciplinary Foundations of the Conceptual Model

Drawing on the review of research published in the four disciplines, the monograph also describes the disciplinary foundations for each of the four layers of the conceptual model and offers examples of research from particular disciplines that are relevant to each layer of the model. Based on our review, we conclude that psychological perspectives dominate the understanding of the "internal context" of student success (Layer One of the model). With their focus on an individual's cognitive and affective processes, psychological perspectives seem ideally suited for understanding how such "core" attributes as an individual's attitudes and motivations influence student success. Although stressing different facets, all four disciplinary perspectives recognize the contribution of the family context (Layer Two of the model) to student success. Economics, sociology, and education perspectives often include attention to the ways that characteristics of the K-12 schools and higher education institutions that students attend (Layer Three of the model) influence student success, while psychological perspectives typically devote less attention to this layer of context. A review of research in these four disciplines also sheds light on the various ways that student success is influenced by the broader social, economic, and policy context (Layer Four).

Implications of the Proposed Model

The persistence of socioeconomic, racial or ethnic, and gender gaps in many dimensions of success suggests that traditional approaches to understanding sources of such gaps are insufficient. Rather than identifying a panacea for raising student success for all students and reducing student success gaps among students, the proposed conceptual model offers a framework for policymakers and practitioners who are interested in working toward these goals. The proposed conceptual framework offers a guide to the development, implementation, and evaluation of policies and practices related to student success. Although existing policies, practices, and research generally focus on discrete aspects of student success, the proposed conceptual model encourages policymakers, practitioners, and researchers to view any student success intervention or indicator as part of a broader and longitudinal student success process. The proposed conceptual model also assumes that incorporating and drawing on multiple theoretical and methodological approaches result in a more complete understanding of the complexity of student success processes and indicators.

The proposed conceptual model offers implications for policymakers and practitioners who seek to improve success for all students and reduce gaps in success among students as well as implications for researchers. For policymakers and practitioners, the model underscores the importance of considering that the effects on student success of any policy or program will likely depend on various aspects of context. Policymakers and practitioners should also recognize that policies and programs do not exist in isolation but interact with both characteristics of other policies and programs as well as the characteristics of the student, family, and school context. Because multiple layers of context inform student success, no one approach will improve student success for all students. Finally, to improve our understanding of the ways that layers of context influence student success, policymakers and practitioners should support a program of research that examines various aspects of the proposed model.

The monograph also offers several recommendations for researchers. Specifically, we recommend that researchers test the extent to which the proposed model may be used to bridge the research and policy or practice communities, incorporate insights from a range of methodological approaches and data sources, understand other indicators of student success, and develop multi- and interdisciplinary approaches to examining student success. Educational researchers may play in advancing both multi- and interdisciplinary approaches as well as overcoming the challenges associated with such research.

Foreword

With a sense of urgency, policymakers, practitioners, and researchers are worried about the current status of postsecondary education in the United States. Amid calls for increasing accountability and the fact of decreasing public funding and support for higher education, those concerned about higher education note significant gaps in access to college and degree attainment associated with racial and ethnic differences and socioeconomic status. They also note concerns about U.S. higher education graduates' faring less well than their counterparts in other countries, lacking key skills needed in the workplace, and entering science, engineering, and mathematics fields in declining numbers—all of it happening in the context of growing tuition costs and declining financial aid available to students (Ewell and Wellman, 2006; Hearn, 2006).

From different vantage points and disciplines, worries about the state of higher education have led many to ask important questions about college student success or the lack thereof. In 2006, the National Postsecondary Education Cooperative (NPEC) organized a symposium and commissioned several papers from national experts on college student success. This monograph is a byproduct of that symposium. The NPEC symposium brought more than 400 individuals from research, policy, and administration backgrounds together to ponder the question of what college student success is and how it should be determined.

What we learn from this monograph is that answering the question—what does it mean to be successful in higher education?—is no simple task. In part, the problem stems from a lack of clarity about the word *success*. Is success about gaining access to college? Is success graduating with a college degree?

Is it the quality and content of student learning? Is it the experiences students have while in college (for example, their engagement or their satisfaction)? Is success about postgraduation outcomes (such as financial gains or professional attainment)? Each of these outcomes could be components of student success, but many other indicators could be used as well. And the difficulty of determining student success is not resolved by simply deciding what success is. Once researchers and policymakers have a sense of what they mean by success, they then face questions about how it might be measured. How should the various definitions of success actually be operationalized? What unit of analysis should be used? Should researchers measure success at the student level, the institutional level, the system level, or across institutions of higher education? How should researchers account for or control the relevant input variables that students possess and the kinds of experiences they had before they got to college? Should studies of student success be longitudinal or cross-sectional? How should researchers isolate the effect that college has on students from other potential influences?

This monograph, written for policymakers, practitioners, and researchers, recognizes that much of the research conducted on student success is based in certain disciplinary perspectives, including sociology, psychology, economics, and education. The authors propose a holistic, interdisciplinary model to examine the complexity of student success in higher education. In the end, they propose a four-level model for understanding student success that involves examining the individual, his or her family origins and influence, the school context, and the larger societal forces. Among the most important points made in this monograph is the idea that policies and programs (at the institutional, state, or federal level) do not operate in a vacuum. The various levels of the model all work together and influence one another, so "fixing" one aspect of a problem might not bring about the desired effect, as since other levels could impede progress.

This monograph joins other recently published ASHE Higher Education monographs on the topic of student success as a means to engage researchers, practitioners, and scholars in a continuing exploration of what it means to help students achieve success in higher education from various perspectives. From *Piecing Together the Student Success Puzzle: Research Propositions and*

Recommendation (ASHE Higher Education Report, volume 32, number 5) on the student success puzzle, to *Economically and Educationally Challenged Students in Higher Education: Access to Outcomes* (ASHE Higher Education Report, volume 33, number 3), to *Reinventing Undergraduate Education: Engaging College Students in Research and Creative Activities* (ASHE Higher Education Report, volume 33, number 4), the ASHE monograph series allows its readers to join the national conversation about student success in higher education. These monographs collectively illustrate that we have a lot of unanswered questions about student success. Monographs like this one are leading us toward answers. They show us the importance of engaging in interdisciplinary, nuanced perspectives and avoiding simplistic one-size-fits-all solutions. These monographs also recognize that fixing what ails higher education demands that we look not just at the student and the institution but also at the larger societal context in which it exists.

Lisa E. Wolf-Wendel
Series Editor

Acknowledgments

This monograph is based on a report that we prepared for the National Postsecondary Education Cooperative's Symposium on Student Success in Washington, D.C., in November 2006. We are grateful for the feedback that we received on this monograph from Jim Hearn, Lisa Wolf-Wendel, and several anonymous reviewers.

Published online in Wiley InterScience
(www.interscience.wiley.com) • DOI: 10.1002/aehe.3401

Introduction

OVER THE PAST FIFTY YEARS, federal and state governments, colleges and universities, and other organizations have developed and supported numerous policies and practices that are designed to promote student success. Among the most extensive and visible efforts are the federally sponsored programs established under the Higher Education Act of 1965, as amended, including the federal Pell grant program, Stafford student loan program, and TRIO programs.

Despite the substantial investment in these and other programs, gaps in student success persist. Regardless of definition, student success varies across groups. For example, rates of college enrollment and bachelor's degree attainment continue to be lower for students from lower-income than higher-income families and for African Americans and Hispanics than for whites (National Center for Education Statistics, 2004). Students from more humble origins are still not only less likely than other students to go to college but, when they do enroll, are also concentrated in lower-quality, less prestigious, and less costly postsecondary educational institutions—postsecondary educational institutions that exhibit lower levels of persistence to the degree and that confer less distinct advantages in the labor market (Thomas and Perna, 2004).

The importance of identifying effective policies and practices for improving success and reducing gaps in success is underscored by projected demographic changes. In short, these projections suggest that the populations that will experience the greatest growth in the coming years will be those that currently experience the lowest levels of student success, that is, students from low-income families and Hispanics (Western Interstate Commission on Higher Education, 2005, 2008). Between 2001–02 and 2021–22, the number of Hispanic public high school graduates is projected to increase by 148 percent, raising the representation of Hispanics among public high school graduates from 12 percent in 2001–02 to 26 percent in 2021–22 (Western Interstate Commission on Higher Education, 2008). At the same time, the number of white public high school graduates is projected to decline by 12 percent, decreasing the representation of whites among public high school graduates from 69 percent in 2001–02 to 52 percent in 2021–22 (Western Interstate Commission on Higher Education, 2008).

Efforts to identify the most effective policies and practices for ensuring success for all students and reducing "success gaps" are limited by at least three forces. First, existing policies and practices generally focus on discrete components, aspects, or predictors of student success with no attention to other forces or processes that also influence student success. In other words, policies and practices are typically developed in isolation, with few comprehensive approaches and little coordination of efforts. For example, student financial aid programs are typically designed to address the inability of some groups to pay for college, with no attention to the other barriers that limit college enrollment and persistence, including inadequate academic preparation. Institutional programs that are designed to promote retention of college students typically focus only on the barriers to persistence with no attention to enrollment processes. Similarly, research generally examines the relationship between particular predictors and discrete measures of student success (the effects of financial aid on college enrollment, for example). As a result, little is known about the relative effectiveness of different approaches or the ways that policies and practices interact to influence student success.

Second, efforts by policymakers, practitioners, and researchers to improve student success are hampered by the absence of a clear, consistent, and comprehensive definition of such success. Numerous books, reports, and journal articles examine various aspects of what might be considered student success. A simple Google search reveals hundreds of items with the phrase "college student success" in the title. The high level of attention to, and range of, outcomes that fall under a student success umbrella is not surprising, given the breadth of outcomes associated with higher education. As an example, Bowen (1997) offers a thoughtful cataloging of the many outcomes of higher education, organizing them under the broad headings of (1) cognitive learning, (2) emotional and moral development, (3) practical competence, (4) direct satisfactions and enjoyment, and (5) avoidance of negative outcomes.

Third, policymakers and practitioners who attempt to use findings from prior research as tools to improve student success must first reconcile the broad array of theoretical and methodological approaches that characterize such research. Research on aspects of student success employs a variety of conceptual frameworks, frameworks that are often defined by particular disciplinary perspectives (for example, sociology, economics, or psychology) and units of analysis (such as students, schools, or states). Certainly the use of numerous theoretical and methodological approaches has the potential benefit of producing a more comprehensive understanding of student success. The diversity of approaches also means, however, that the body of research on student success is characterized by wide-ranging, and sometimes inconsistent, findings. The unwieldiness and inconsistency necessarily frustrate attempts to identify, develop, and sustain a program of policies and practices that may raise the level of success for all students and lead to a reduction in student success gaps.

Purpose of This Monograph

Based on its review of student success research, the Social Science Research Council (SSRC) noted the need "for a more conceptual and reflective approach to notions of access, retention, success, and opportunity that takes into account the multiple pathways that individuals take to postsecondary attainment and acknowledges the variability of how these terms are defined by different consumers, communities, and policymakers" (2005, p. 21). This monograph addresses this need by proposing an overarching conceptual framework that policymakers, practitioners, and researchers may use to guide the development, implementation, and evaluation of policies and practices for improving success for all students and reducing persisting racial, ethnic, and socioeconomic gaps in student success. The framework does not provide a model for understanding any specific student success outcome or stage, but it is designed to bring order to the wide array of theoretical and methodological approaches that, only when considered together, provide a comprehensive understanding of the ways that policymakers and practitioners may more usefully intervene to effectively promote student success. In short, the model is a tool for understanding the ways that multiple areas of research can be brought together to generate a more comprehensive and complete understanding of student success processes for different groups of students.

After describing our approach and procedures, the monograph presents the results of a multidisciplinary examination of the theoretical and methodological approaches that researchers have used to inform knowledge and understanding of student success. Then the monograph presents and describes a conceptual model for tying these perspectives together. The monograph concludes with recommended uses of the proposed model for policy, practice, and further research.

Our Approach

Our approach to developing this framework assumes the centrality of disciplinary perspectives for understanding student success. Disciplines bring specific methods for identifying, conceptualizing, and analyzing questions of student success. In every discipline, research design, data collection, and analysis reflect a researcher's response to a number of underlying philosophical questions that define what might be seen and what might be ignored in the inquiry. These epistemological elements are fundamentally related to disciplinary identities themselves.

Recognizing the value of disciplinary perspectives, this monograph is designed to promote a better understanding of similarities and differences in disciplinary perspectives of student success to show how, when considered together, disciplinary perspectives create redundancies and gaps in our understanding of student success. Because disciplinary norms guide decisions about appropriate foci, conceptual frames, and empirical approaches, we expect disciplinary variance in perspectives and conclusions about student success.

Guided in part by the results of the SSRC review (2005), this monograph focuses on four disciplines with high levels of scholarly attention to indicators of student success: economics, psychology, sociology, and education. Economic theory explains the ways students make decisions to invest various resources in their postsecondary education. Psychological theories describe the ways students' attitudes, motivations, and goals shape their behaviors. Sociology includes functional, critical, and interactionist theories that describe social forces that advantage some students while disadvantaging others. Education draws on theories and frameworks from across disciplines to examine various indicators of student success.

To develop the framework, we rely on the literature, not for a traditional review and synthesis of predictors of discrete indicators of student success, but for a description of the characteristics of and approaches to the research that has been conducted in each of these four disciplines. Our intention is not to update or replicate the excellent substantive syntheses that exist (for example, Feldman and Newcomb, 1969; Pascarella and Terenzini, 1993, 2005). Instead, this monograph complements these syntheses of "how college affects students" by developing a framework for understanding how different disciplinary perspectives can be used together to more completely inform our understanding of student success processes.

Definition of Student Success

A first step in understanding the contribution of different disciplinary perspectives is to define student success. Reflecting our goal of identifying a framework that is useful to policymakers, practitioners, and researchers, we operationalize student success as completion or effective exercise of one of ten indicators of educational attainment. Figure 1 shows that these ten indicators represent four key transitions in a longitudinal student success process. The first transition involves becoming "ready" for college and is measured by educational aspirations or expectations and academic preparation for college. The second transition is marked by enrollment into college and is measured by college access and college choice. The third transition, college achievement, is represented by academic performance in college, transfer among institutions, and persistence to program or degree completion. The final transition, postcollege attainment, is measured by enrollment in graduate and professional schools, income, and educational attainment.

FIGURE 1
Transitions and Indicators of Student Success

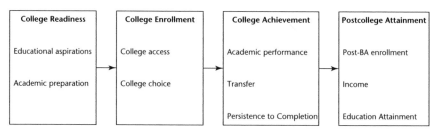

College Readiness	College Enrollment	College Achievement	Postcollege Attainment
Educational aspirations	College access	Academic performance	Post-BA enrollment
Academic preparation	College choice	Transfer	Income
		Persistence to Completion	Education Attainment

Our decision to operationalize student success using these ten indicators of educational attainment is consistent with the weight that policymakers give to these measures in accountability systems. For example, in its state-by-state report card, the National Center for Public Policy and Higher Education (2006) awards grades to states in the following categories: academic preparation for success in college, participation and enrollment in college, affordability, persistence and degree completion, and benefits (for example, educational attainment, income, and other benefits). Although learning is also a stated category, most states received an "incomplete," reflecting the National Center's conclusion that appropriate indicators of this outcome do not currently exist for all states.

This definition of student success emphasizes certain outcomes over others. In other words, this definition of student success implies that all students should enroll in college, persist to program or degree completion, enroll in and complete advanced degree programs, and earn high incomes. Not all individuals have, should have, or will ever have these goals. Nonetheless, many policies and practices are directed toward achieving these outcomes, and, despite these efforts, the shares of students who accomplish these outcomes vary systematically across socioeconomic, racial and ethnic, and gender groups. Indeed, much existing work on student success outcomes describes wide variance in these distributions.

This definition of student success has other limitations. Defining student success in terms of these discrete outcomes oversimplifies the work of postsecondary educational institutions. Moreover, despite its breadth, the list of ten indicators of student success is not exhaustive. These indicators exclude numerous other attributes and outcomes that may characterize a "successful" student and have policy significance, including academic preparation before high school, choice of major field, career search activities, and choice of career field.

Nonetheless, attention to every possible indicator of student success is beyond the scope of any one monograph. Moreover, the overarching purpose of this monograph is not to develop a model that is specific to any one particular indicator but that may be used to improve our understanding of student success processes more generally. Therefore, although based on a specific and limited list of outcomes, the proposed framework may be generalizable to a wider range of outcomes, especially those that may mediate the outcomes that are considered in this monograph.

Procedures

We developed the proposed conceptual model based on a review of research examining the ten indicators of success in each of the four selected disciplines: economics, sociology, psychology, and education. With the goal of capitalizing on the best existing thinking and research on student success, we limited the review to articles that examined one of the ten indicators of success and that were published in top journals in the four disciplines.

We limited the review to articles published in top journals for several reasons. First, we assume that the articles that are published in these journals represent the topics, theoretical perspectives, and methodological approaches on which there is the greatest agreement among scholars in the field. Second, because we are not trained in all disciplines, we wanted to apply a uniform and systematic set of procedures for selecting articles to include. Finally, attention only to the top journals limits the scope of the review, increasing its manageability. As with all selection criteria, however, these criteria necessarily exclude a substantial share of research in each of the four disciplines. Most important, this review likely underestimates the contribution of "minority" viewpoints, that is, topics, theoretical perspectives, and methodological approaches outside the disciplinary mainstream and less widely embraced.

Exhibits 1 and 2 list the journals in each discipline that we reviewed for relevant articles. We examined journal articles on each of these indicators that

EXHIBIT 1
Top Journals by Discipline, as Measured by Citations and Impact Factor, 2003

Discipline	Journal	Citations	(rank)	Impact Factor	(rank)	Recognized by Other Source
Education	Review of Educational Research	1,323	(1)	1.69	(1)	O'Brien (2001)
	American Educational Research Journal	1,175	(3)	1.64	(2)	O'Brien (2001)
Psychology, Educational	Child Development	12,358	(1)	3.32	(1)	Burgard (2001)
	Journal of Educational Psychology	3,892	(2)	1.52	(9)	O'Brien (2001)
	Journal of Counseling Psychology	2,084	(3)	1.54	(8)	Burgard (2001)
Psychology, Applied	Journal of Applied Psychology	7,246	(1)	2.17	(1)	Burgard (2001)
	Organizational Behavior and Human Decision Processes	3,124	(2)	1.43	(9)	Burgard (2001)
Psychology, Developmental	Child Development	12,358	(1)	3.32	(4)	Burgard (2001)
	Developmental Psychology	7,520	(3)	3.32	(8)	Burgard (2001)
Psychology, Social	Journal of Personality and Social Psychology	25,072	(1)	3.86	(2)	Burgard (2001)
	Personality and Social Psychology Bulletin	4,101	(2)	1.84	(8)	Burgard (2001)
Sociology	American Sociological Review	5,607	(1)	2.38	(2)	Garand and Giles (2003)
	American Journal of Sociology	4,980	(2)	2.33	(3)	Garand and Giles (2003)
	Annual Review of Sociology	1,651	(5)	3.21	(1)	
Economics	American Economic Review	11,935	(1)	1.94	(8)	Garand and Giles (2003)
	Econometrica	9,775	(2)	2.22	(10)	

Source: Analyses of ISI Web of Knowledge, 2003.

EXHIBIT 2
Journals Specializing in Higher Education by Number of Citations and Impact Factor, 2003

Discipline	Journal	Citations	(rank)	Impact Factor	(rank)	Recognized by Other Source
Education	*Journal of Higher Education*	400	(22)	0.38	(51)	O'Brien (2001)
	Review of Higher Education	169	(59)	0.39	(49)	O'Brien (2001)
Sociology	*Sociology of Education*	728	(11)	1.05	(14)	O'Brien (2001)
Economics	*Economics of Education Review*	407	(73)	0.47	(97)	

Source: Analyses of ISI Web of Knowledge, 2003.

were published between January 1, 1995, and June 30, 2005. We identified these top journals using several approaches. First, we used the ISI *2003 Journal Citation Reports, Social Sciences Edition* to identify journals with both the highest numbers of citations and highest "impact factors." The *Journal Citation Reports* define the "impact factor" as the ratio of the number of citations in 2003 to articles published in 2001 and 2002 relative to the total number of articles published in 2001 and 2002.

Second, because citations are an imperfect method of assessing journal quality, we also consulted articles that discuss the relative importance of journals in different fields. In most cases these articles confirmed the selection of top journals. For example, in education, *Review of Educational Research* and *American Educational Research Journal* have higher numbers of citations and impact factors than virtually any other journal in education or educational research (ISI Web of Knowledge, 2003). Similarly, O'Brien (2001) labels *American Educational Research Journal* and *Review of Educational Research* as "journal[s] of the century" in educational research.

We also examined articles published on student success in two journals that focus specifically on education (*Economics of Education Review* and

Sociology of Education) as well as two journals that focus specifically on higher education (*Journal of Higher Education* and *Review of Higher Education*). Although these specialized journals have lower numbers of citations and lower impact factors than the top disciplinary journals (see Exhibit 2), other sources recognize the contribution of these publications. For example, in her review of "journals of the century in education," O'Brien (2001) concluded that Journal of Higher Education is "a key journal for providing scholarly research and practice papers related to postsecondary education" (p. 97) and that *Review of Higher Education* "provides a respected forum for essays, articles, and reviews" (pp. 97–98).

Conclusion

Federal, state, and local policymakers, K-12 and college administrators, and numerous researchers have invested substantial effort into improving and reducing gaps in student success. But these efforts are hampered, at least in part, by the wide array of theoretical and methodological approaches that characterize such research.

This monograph attempts to bring order to the unwieldiness of these multiple but generally discrete approaches by developing an overarching model for understanding student success. This chapter outlines our approach to developing the conceptual model, including our assumption that disciplinary perspectives are central to any understanding of student success and our procedures for identifying these disciplinary perspectives. The next chapter summarizes the conclusions that we draw from our review of research published in four disciplines and proposes a conceptual model for understanding student success that builds on these conclusions.

A Conceptual Model for Understanding Disciplinary Approaches to Student Success

USING THE PROCEDURES OUTLINED IN THE PREVIOUS chapter, this chapter begins by describing six conclusions about disciplinary approaches to student success. Building on these conclusions, the chapter concludes by proposing a multilayered conceptual model for understanding student success and outlines the model's underlying assumptions.

Disciplinary Approaches to Student Success

From our review of research on student success published in top journals in each of the four disciplines, we draw the following six conclusions about disciplinary approaches to student success:

1. Theoretical approaches to understanding student success vary across the four disciplines;
2. The relative attention to student success in articles published in top journals varies across disciplines;
3. Even within disciplines, aspects of student success that are examined vary;
4. Methodological approaches and sources of data for exploring student success vary across disciplines and, as one might expect, are rather tightly bound to the theoretical stance employed;
5. The unit of analysis varies by disciplinary and theoretical approach; and
6. Attention to differences in student success across groups varies across the four disciplines.

The chapter discusses each of these conclusions in turn.

Variations Across Disciplines in Theoretical Approaches to Student Success

Each discipline offers a distinct array of theoretical approaches to understanding student success. Exhibit 3 summarizes the relative prevalence of different theoretical approaches in each of the four disciplines.

EXHIBIT 3
Theoretical Perspectives Used to Examine Student Success in Articles in Top Journals in Various Disciplines

Discipline	Theories and Constructs	Number of Articles
Psychology	Achievement motivation and goal theory	12
	Stereotype threat	11
	Parenting practices and relationships	6
	Personality traits (Big Five, self-efficacy)	2
	Control (perceived academic control, control-mastery, self-determination)	3
	Perceived social/cultural context	2
	Psychopathology, stress, test anxiety	3
	Cognitive theories	5
	Attributional style	1
	Hope theory	1
	Interpersonal competence	1
	Self-enhancement bias	1
	Social comparisons	1
	Social dominance theory	1
	Test/construct validity	1
	Tinto's model of academic and social integration	1
	Other (including not articulated)	4
Sociology*	Cultural reproduction (capital)	10
	Human capital	2
	Status attainment	7
	Social network	2
	Marginality theory	1
	Symbolic interaction	1
	Self-efficacy	1

EXHIBIT 3 *(Continued)*

Economics*	Human capital theory	32
	Consumer theory	7
	Economics—broadly	17
Education	Economic:	
	Economic model of determinants of income	1
	Economic theories of public sector	1
	Expected utility	1
	Human capital	2
	Sociological:	
	Habitus and cultural capital	7
	Bourdieuian field analysis	1
	Network	1
	Psychological:	
	Cognition and metacognition	1
	Motivation and cognition	2
	Predictive validity	1
	Self-efficacy	1
	Social cognitive theory of self-regulation	1
	Public policy:	
	Affirmative action rationales	1
	Multiple theories:	
	Human capital + social and cultural capital	3
	Human capital + consumer theory	2
	Conceptual models:	
	Three-phase model of college choice	2
	I-E-O	2
	Involvement "theory"	1
	Tinto's model of student departure	8
	Tipping point theory	1
	Weidmann's socialization model	1
	Bean social integration model	2
	No theory articulated	25

*At least one study in this area employs multiple theoretical perspectives; thus, the totals will exceed the total number of publications listed in Exhibit 3.

Economics. When examining the ten indicators of student success, neoclassical economists generally focus on understanding the ways that individuals allocate resources to maximize their interests. Exhibit 3 shows that the most common economic perspectives for understanding student success draw on human capital theory (thirty-two of the fifty economics articles). A smaller number of articles (seven) use consumer theory. Although behavioral economists attend to the cognitive and emotional elements of decision making, few economics articles use these perspectives to examine student success. Most economists working with success indicators rely on assumptions found in rational choice theory—assumptions that obviate direct examinations of the underlying cognitive dimensions of individuals' choices.

The microeconomic theory framing much of the work on student success indicators assumes the existence of rational actors who can identify a range of outcomes and associate each with a value (money and time, for example). Economists debate this assumption of actor rationality, as shown by a cursory review of the literature on bounded rationality (for example, Simon, 1957; March 1994; Elster 1983; Gigerenzer and Selton 2001).

Consumer theory deals with the ways that economic agents (such as students) prioritize, and ultimately choose between, real or imagined alternatives. These choices involve economic concepts of indifference and budget constraint, income, and availability of substitutes. Consumer theory is often used in research that examines the relationship between affordability and such indicators of student success as enrollment and persistence (see, for example, Siegfried and Getz, 2006).

Human capital theory is frequently used to guide economic inquiry focusing on the private economic returns to education (see, for example, Averett and Burton, 1996; Monks, 1997). Though almost universally attributed to Becker (1993) and Mincer (1974), the human capital model taps the fundamental ideas laid out by Marx's notions (1891) of labor-power. As human capital theory assumes that when individuals invest in their stock of skills they will be rewarded in the labor market, Marx's labor-power concept outlines the ways that workers sell their labor through the workforce.

Although a dominant frame in much of the literature in economics, human capital has several weaknesses for examinations of student success indicators.

First, the traditional human capital framework relies on signals such as educational credentials to provide employers with a gauge of an individual's potential value. Such signals have been shown to be loosely coupled with the general and specific knowledge assumed to be valued by employers (Becker, 1993). Second, traditional human capital theory ignores market imperfections that are manifest in realities such as race and gender discrimination (Leontaridi, 1998). A third challenge for the rational-actor model in economics deals with the availability of information in decision making (Gintis, 1978). Little direct attention to these issues is paid in the economics literature on the ten student success indicators.

Sociology. Although including attention to a number of theoretical perspectives, Exhibit 3 shows that a plurality of sociology journal articles use cultural reproduction theories (ten of the twenty-four sociology articles). Although the field of social psychology and work in the area of symbolic interaction often consider cognitive processes that inform human behavior, these perspectives are used in only a small number of articles on student success in our review (one article involving symbolic interaction; one article involving marginality theory).

Theories of cultural reproduction focus on the ways that familial and class advantage are transferred from generation to generation, thus strengthening advantages enjoyed by previous generations and further stratifying the broader society. Strictly considered, cultural reproduction models treat social class as a primary determinant of children's future status and often cast education as a means by which existing class structures are reinforced rather than relaxed. For example, reproductionists point out that poor children are more likely to be systematically exposed to educational experiences that shape their expectations and behaviors in ways that prepare them for lower-status occupations than their more affluent peers who receive qualitatively different (that is, superior) educational training and community support. Some of the most highly regarded sociologists (such as Coleman and others, 1964) have devoted significant attention to the role of education in social stratification and occupational attainment processes. Despite the prevalence of reproductive frameworks in this research, the vast majority of contemporary studies in sociology journals affirm the democratizing effect of education; that is, most of the published work either assumes that education is capable of overcoming class constraints or explicitly models the ways that this process occurs for students at different positions in the class structure.

Undergirding much of the evolution in sociological thinking about the role of the family is a corpus of work surrounding the writing of French sociologists Jean-Claude Passeron and Pierre Bourdieu. Their seminal work *Cultural Reproduction and Social Reproduction* (1973) developed the idea of cultural capital-forms of skill, knowledge, or education that give advantage vis-à-vis higher status in society–and cultural reproduction, the process through which social status is passed on through generations. Passeron and Bourdieu argued that education played a critical role in the transmission of generational advantage and disadvantage and that this transmission was key to capitalist societies that required a stratified social system.

An element of sociological theories about the role of the family in student success is *habitus*—a complex concept describing the combined environmental effects (family, home, school, church, community, and so forth) on one's view of place in society. Focusing on gender differences in K–12 cocurricular engagement, Dumais (2002) provides a good example of the ways that family environments influence the K–12 activities that are directly related to college going.

Although the education literature includes invocations of the habitus concept, the absence of direct references to this construct in the sociological literature likely reflects at least two major concerns. First, as Dumais (2002) and Kingston (2001) point out, the concept of habitus is ill defined theoretically, thereby limiting proper measurement. Second, and perhaps more problematic, many have questioned the applicability of the concept of cultural capital in the United States—a nation-state decidedly less class based than France of the 1960s (see Lamont and Lareau, 1988, for a critique on this dimension).

More common in sociology are articles that draw from a more generalized version of cultural reproduction (for example, Karen, 2002; Schleef, 2000). Schleef highlights the importance of parental occupational status and the transmission of associated values to maintaining cross-generational social status. Karen illuminates the contribution of family and cultural influences to the quality of students' college choice sets. Both Schleef and Karen demonstrate the importance of family to educational attainment and maintenance of social class position.

Psychology. As a discipline, psychology comprises many subfields and specialties, including applied, developmental, educational, and social. In general, psychologists are interested in understanding the influences on student success of cognitive processes and attitudes. Exhibit 3 shows that the most common theoretical perspectives for informing psychological examinations of student success are achievement motivation and goal theory (twelve articles) and stereotype threat (eleven articles).

A substantial share of psychology articles adopts an achievement motivation or goal theory approach. This perspective generally assumes that academic performance is influenced by students' achievement goals and that achievement goals are a product of personality traits, particularly achievement motivations. The two primary types of achievement goals are mastery/work goals and performance/competitiveness goals, although some researchers also consider performance avoidance/fear of failure goals. Achievement motivation theories generally assume, and research generally shows, that students who are motivated to master or learn material tend to adopt mastery goals, while students who are motivated to demonstrate competence or better achievement than their peers adopt performance goals (see, for example, Harackiewicz and others, 2000; Harackiewicz, Barron, Tauer, and Elliot, 2002). Students who fear failure tend to adopt performance avoidance goals, exerting minimal effort to complete requirements.

Education. Not surprisingly, journal articles in education draw on theoretical perspectives from various disciplines, particularly sociology (nine of sixty-two articles). Smaller numbers draw on psychological theories (six articles) and economic theories (five articles). The most common sociological perspectives used in educational journals draw on notions of habitus and cultural capital (seven of the nine articles), while the most common economic perspectives employ human capital theory (two of the five articles) and the most common psychological perspectives involve aspects of cognitive theories (four of six articles).

Likely reflecting the applied nature of the field, a notable share of articles published in education journals use only a conceptual model, not a theoretical approach (seventeen articles). A guiding theoretical perspective is not articulated in twenty-five articles in educational journals.

A small number of articles published in education journals draw on a conceptual model that reflects multiple theoretical perspectives. Focused on indicators of student college choice, these studies stress the strengths of models that incorporate aspects of economic human capital and sociological notions of cultural and social capital (see, for example, Freeman, 1997; Perna, 2000, 2004). A conceptual model that draws on both economic and sociological perspectives assumes that students' educational decisions are determined, at least in part, by their habitus, or the system of values and beliefs that shapes an individual's views and interpretations (Paulsen and St. John, 2002; Perna, 2000, 2004; St. John, Paulsen, and Carter, 2005).

Both qualitative and quantitative research demonstrates the merits of using an integrated conceptual model for examining enrollment decisions. Freeman's qualitative study (1997) revealed that African American high school students believe that both economic and sociocultural factors restrict the college enrollment of African Americans. Specifically, Freeman found that African American high school students were uncertain about their ability to pay the short-term costs of attending college and about whether the long-term economic benefits of attending would exceed the costs, that is, elements of a human capital investment model. Interviewees also pointed to the potential influence of structural barriers (for example, physical conditions of the schools attended by African Americans), social capital (such as interest and assistance from teachers, counselors, and African American role models), and cultural capital (believing at an early age that pursuing postsecondary education is a realistic option, for example).

By reflecting differences in expectations, preferences, tastes, and certainty about higher education investment decisions, measures of social and cultural capital appear to be particularly important for understanding differences across groups in college enrollment decisions that are not explained by human capital investment models. Using logistic regression analyses of data from the National Educational Longitudinal Study, Perna (2000) found that measures of social and cultural capital improved the explanatory power of a traditional econometric model of college enrollment that included only measures of gender, race, financial resources, and academic preparation and achievement. Moreover, measures of cultural and social capital played a relatively more important role in explaining the college enrollment decisions of African Americans and Hispanics than of whites (Perna, 2000).

Variations in Attention to Student Success

Attention to student success, as measured by the frequency of relevant articles published in top journals, varies across disciplines. Exhibit 4 shows the number of articles in each journal in each discipline that examined at least one of our ten indicators of student success between January 1, 1995, and June 30, 2005. The exhibit shows that the number of relevant articles varies across disciplines, ranging from twenty-four in sociology to fifty in economics, fifty-six in psychology, and sixty-two in education.

Attention to the ten student success indicators varies not only across the four disciplines but also in the top journals in each discipline. Nearly all the economics articles are from one of the three journals reviewed, *Economics of Education Review* (forty-five of the fifty articles in economics). Of the four journals in sociology, *Sociology of Education* accounts for twenty of the twenty-four articles on student success indicators that were published over this time period. In psychology, two of the eight journals reviewed accounted for a disproportionate share of the fifty-six total articles: *Journal of Educational Psychology* (seventeen) and *Journal of Personality and Social Psychology* (sixteen). Relatively few of the articles published in the applied psychology journals (seven of the fifty-six psychology articles) or the developmental psychology journals (seven of the fifty-six) examined the ten student success indicators. In education, the ten student success indicators are a more common focus of the *Review of Higher Education* (twenty-seven articles) and *Journal of Higher Education* (twenty-four articles) than of the *Review of Educational Research* (six articles) and *American Educational Research Journal* (five articles).

Variations in Aspects of Student Success Examined

A review of the literature published in top journals also reveals variation in relative attention to different aspects of student success. Together, articles in different disciplines and areas cover the range of student success indicators that mark students' success through the four transitions, from college readiness to college entrance, college achievement, and postcollege attainment transitions.

EXHIBIT 4
Number of Articles That Examined an Indicator of Student Success Published in Top Journals Between January 1, 1995, and June 30, 2005

Discipline	Journal	Number of Articles
Education	Total	62
	Review of Educational Research	6
	American Educational Research Journal	5
	Journal of Higher Education	24
	Review of Higher Education	27
Psychology	Total	56
Educational Psychology	*Journal of Educational Psychology*	17
	Journal of Counseling Psychology	5
Applied Psychology	*Journal of Applied Psychology*	7
	Organizational Behavior and Human Decision Processes	0
Developmental Psychology	*Child Development*	3
	Developmental Psychology	4
Social Psychology	*Journal of Personality and Social Psychology*	16
	Personality and Social Psychology Bulletin	4
Sociology	Total	24
	American Sociological Review	2
	American Journal of Sociology	0
	Annual Review of Sociology	2
	Sociology of Education	20
Economics	Total	50
	American Economic Review	4
	Econometrica	1
	Economics of Education Review	45

The most frequently examined student success indicator in the literature we reviewed for this monograph was academic performance during college (seventy articles), followed by college access and enrollment (thirty-nine articles) and persistence or degree completion (thirty-two articles). Academic performance is a particularly common indicator in psychology journals.

Exhibit 5 shows that forty of the seventy articles examining academic performance were in psychology journals. Education journals also include substantial attention to academic performance in college (twenty-one articles), while sociology (six articles) and economics (three journals) include relatively little attention to this indicator.

College access or enrollment is the most common student success indicator in economics (sixteen articles) and sociology (eleven articles) journals. Income or earnings is the second most common indicator in economics journals (eleven articles). Persistence, the third most frequently examined indicator, is a relatively more common area of interest in education (fifteen articles) and economics (ten articles) than in other disciplines.

Variations in Methodological Approaches and Sources of Data

Regardless of discipline, the most common methodological approach in articles examining student success published in the selected journals is quantitative rather than qualitative. Exhibit 6 shows that 175 articles used quantitative methodologies. Only ten articles used qualitative methodologies, and twelve articles were literature reviews. Qualitative methodologies are relatively more common in education (five of the sixty-two articles in education) and sociology (four of the twenty-four articles in sociology) than in psychology (one of the fifty-six articles in psychology) and economics (none of the fifty articles in economics).

Quantitative methodologies may be classified into three paradigms: descriptive, correlational, and causal. The most common quantitative research design in research examining student success is correlational, involving such analytic techniques as regression analyses, path analyses, and structural equation modeling. Across the four disciplines, 149 articles used correlational designs. Correlational designs are especially common in articles published in education journals (fifty of sixty-two articles), sociology journals (sixteen of twenty-four articles), and economics journals (forty-eight of fifty articles). A smaller share of articles in psychology used correlational designs (thirty-five of fifty-six articles).

Within the correlational paradigm are quantitative studies concerned with particular statistical issues. For example, a small number of the psychology articles focused on assessing the psychometric properties of measures, including measures of biographical data (Oswald and others, 2004) and race-based

EXHIBIT 5
Student Success Outcomes Examined in Articles in Top Journals in Various Disciplines Between January 1, 1995, and June 30, 2005

Outcome	Discipline	Number of Articles
Academic preparation for college	Total	9
	Education	1
	Psychology	5
	Sociology	0
	Economics	3
Educational aspirations	Total	21
	Education	9
	Psychology	6
	Sociology	2
	Economics	4
College access or enrollment	Total	39
	Education	11
	Psychology	1
	Sociology	11
	Economics	16
College choice	Total	14
	Education	7
	Psychology	1
	Sociology	1
	Economics	5
Academic performance	Total	70
	Education	21
	Psychology	40
	Sociology	6
	Economics	3
Persistence/degree completion	Total	32
	Education	15
	Psychology	4
	Sociology	3
	Economics	10

EXHIBIT 5 *(Continued)*

Graduate school enrollment	Total	15
	Education	10
	Psychology	0
	Sociology	2
	Economics	3
Income or earnings	Total	17
	Education	2
	Psychology	0
	Sociology	4
	Economics	11
Educational attainment	Total	9
	Education	0
	Psychology	2
	Sociology	5
	Economics	2

Note: Some studies examine more than one outcome.

rejection sensitivity (Mendoza-Denton and others, 2002). In economics, four articles focused on improving statistical estimations of relationships driving indicators of student success. These economics articles demonstrate the implications of failing to statistically address such issues as self-selection (see, for example, Arias and McMahon, 2001; Ichimura and Taber, 2002).

Experimental designs—that is, designs that generate conclusions about causal relationships—are relatively common among articles published in psychology journals but rare in journals in other disciplines. Exhibit 6 shows that fifteen articles in psychology (about one-fourth of the fifty-six psychology articles) use experimental designs. A notable share of articles in psychology journals include two or three studies, including five articles with at least one study using a correlational design and one using an experimental design (Barron and Harackiewicz, 2001; Brown and others, 2000; Cullen, Hardison, and Sackett, 2004; Ford, Ferguson, Brooks, and Hagadone, 2004; Robins and Beer, 2001). In contrast with the relative prevalence in psychology, only one article in education (Nagda and others, 1998) used an experimental design

EXHIBIT 6
Methodological Approaches to Student Success in Articles in Top Journals in Various Disciplines

Method	Discipline	Number of Articles
Descriptive	Total	9
	Education	4
	Psychology	5
	Sociology	0
	Economics	0
Correlational	Total	149
	Education	50
	Psychology	35
	Sociology	16
	Economics	48
Causal/experimental	Total	17
	Education	1
	Psychology	15*
	Sociology	0
	Economics	1
Qualitative	Total	10
	Education	5
	Psychology	1
	Sociology	4
	Economics	0
Literature review	Total	12
	Education	6
	Psychology	0
	Sociology	4
	Economics	1

*Note: Five of the psychology articles in this category include at least two studies, at least one that uses experimental design and one that uses a correlational design.

with random assignment of students to treatment and control conditions. A single quasi-experimental design was identified in the economics literature (Dynarski, 2002). None of the articles in the sociology journals in our review employed an experimental design.

Reflecting the range of research designs, the sources of data also vary across the four disciplines. Consistent with the applied nature of the field, articles in education journals generally draw on a broader range of sources of data than articles in psychology, sociology, and economics. Educational research includes use of the large-scale national datasets sponsored by the U. S. Department of Education (for example, the National Educational Longitudinal Survey of 1988 eighth graders, Beginning Postsecondary Student Survey, Baccalaureate and Beyond) as well as the Cooperative Institutional Research Program sponsored by UCLA's Higher Education Research Initiative. Other studies use data from the Integrated Postsecondary Education Data System, other multi-institutional samples (such as the National Study of Student Learning [Pascarella, Wolniak, Flowers and Peirson, 2004]), and state systems of higher education. A smaller number of quantitative studies draw on data from a single institution, while qualitative studies use purposively selected samples of students (see, for example, Freeman, 1999; Fries-Britt and Turner, 2002).

Psychology articles tend to use data from students attending a single institution, with a substantial share of studies drawing data from students enrolled in sections of one course (such as introductory psychology). One article in psychology involved testing hypotheses about gender differences in the relationship between spatial skills and mathematics performance using four different samples of students (Casey, Nuttall, Pezaris, and Benbow, 1995). A smaller number of psychology studies use multi-institutional but not national samples such as African American students attending four public high schools in one school district (Chavous and others, 2003), students attending high schools in California and Wisconsin (Glasgow and others, 1997), and students with SAT and college grade data attending thirteen institutions (Cullen, Hardison, and Sackett, 2004).

In economics and sociology, virtually all studies capitalize on the availability of data from a small number of national surveys of students. Among the most common sources of data in both sociology and economics journal articles are national datasets sponsored by the U. S. Department of Education, particularly the Beginning Postsecondary Student survey, National Educational Longitudinal Study of 1988 eighth graders, and High School and Beyond. A smaller share of studies draw on data from the National Longitudinal Study of Youth, the Panel Study of Income Dynamics, and the Current Population Survey.

When appropriately weighted, national datasets provide information about nationally representative samples of students. Explicit attention to issues of weighting and sample design varied across the areas we reviewed. Articles in economics and sociology were more attentive to explicit consideration of weighting issues than was the research using secondary data in education. Sample design issues, another biasing side effect of large-scale secondary datasets, was rarely addressed in the literature that we reviewed (see Thomas and Heck, 2001, or Stapleton and Thomas, 2008, for an overview of associated biases).

Although relatively uncommon in sociological journals, a notable share of articles in economics journals used institutional data. For example, Ehrenberg and Smith (2004) used data from the higher education system in the state of New York, Singell (2004) used data from Oregon colleges, and Kerkvliet and Nowell (2005) used data from institutions in Oregon and Utah. While providing more limited generalizability, institutional data may enable greater precision in model specification and greater depth of variables than national data.

Variations Across Disciplines in the Unit of Analysis

The student is the typical unit of analysis in research examining the ten student success indicators. Exhibit 7 shows that virtually all the articles in education (fifty-five of sixty-two), psychology (fifty-six of fifty-six), sociology (twenty of twenty-four), and economics (forty-six of fifty) used the student as the unit of analysis.

Although all the psychology articles used the student as the unit of analysis, a small number of articles in other disciplines use units of analysis other than the student. Exhibit 7 shows that one education article and two economics articles used the institution as the unit of analysis, while one education article and one economics article used the state as the unit of analysis.

One article in education used multiple units of analysis (for example, student and state). Perna and Titus (2004) used multilevel analyses to account for the inclusion of both the student and the state as units of analysis and found that measures of four types of state public policies (direct appropriations to higher education institutions, tuition, financial aid to students, and elementary and secondary education) were related to the college enrollment patterns of 1992 high school graduates.

EXHIBIT 7
Unit of Analysis in Articles in Top Journals in Various Disciplines

Method	Discipline	Number of Articles
Student	Total	177
	Education	55
	Psychology	56
	Sociology	20
	Economics	46
Institution	Total	3
	Education	1
	Psychology	0
	Sociology	0
	Economics	2
State	Total	2
	Education	1
	Psychology	0
	Sociology	0
	Economics	1
Study	Total	10
	Education	5
	Psychology	0
	Sociology	4
	Economics	1
Multiple	Total	3
	Education	1
	Psychology	0
	Sociology	1
	Economics	1

Variations in Attention to Differences Across Groups

Articles in top journals also vary across disciplines in terms of their relative attention to understanding differences in student success across groups and the level of attention devoted to different groups. Exhibit 8 shows that attention to variations in student success across groups is relatively common in education

EXHIBIT 8
Attention to Differences Across Groups in Articles Published in Top Journals in Various Disciplines

Method	Discipline	Number of Articles
Gender	Total	53
	Education	13
	Psychology	22
	Sociology	9
	Economics	9
Race/ethnicity	Total	49
	Education	18
	Psychology	9
	Sociology	10
	Economics	12
Socioeconomic status	Total	51
	Education	17
	Psychology	0
	Sociology	16
	Economics	18
Institution	Total	35
	Education	13
	Psychology	0
	Sociology	6
	Economics	16

articles, with sixty-one examinations of subgroup differences. Education articles include roughly equal levels of attention to differences in student success by gender (thirteen articles), race/ethnicity (eighteen articles), socioeconomic status (seventeen articles), and institutional type (thirteen articles).

Across all four disciplines, gender, socioeconomic status, and race or ethnicity are the most common foci of subgroup examinations, as gender differences were examined in fifty-three articles, socioeconomic status in fifty-one articles, and race or ethnicity in forty-nine articles. Psychology articles account for nearly half the examinations of differences in student success by gender (twenty-two of fifty-three articles). Of the thirty-one psychology articles that included examinations of group differences, the majority (twenty-two) focused on gender differences and the remainder (nine) focused on differences across racial or ethnic groups.

Although none of the psychology articles examined differences by socio-economic status, socioeconomic status differences were a focus in seventeen education articles, sixteen sociology articles, and eighteen economics articles. Differences in student success across racial or ethnic groups are a relatively more common area of interest in education (eighteen) than in psychology (nine), sociology (ten), and economics (twelve).

A smaller number of articles examine differences in student success based on the characteristics of the higher education institution attended. Exhibit 8 shows that thirty-five articles include attention to this source of differences. Differences in student success by institutional type are relatively more common in economics (sixteen articles) and education (thirteen articles) than in psychology (no articles) and sociology (six articles).

Proposed Conceptual Model of Student Success

Clearly research on student success is characterized by a range of theoretical and methodological approaches, with differences largely reflecting particular disciplinary perspectives. We propose a conceptual model for understanding student success that reflects the central conclusions from our review of different disciplinary approaches to student success. This model incorporates both commonalities and differences across theoretical and methodological approaches to student success into an overarching conceptual model. Whereas a theory is "a system for explaining a set of phenomena by specifying constructs and the laws that relate these constructs to each other" (Borg and Gall, 1989, p. 25), a conceptual model is a specification derived from a body of research about the relationships among variables.

An expansion and refinement of the conceptual model that Perna (2006a) developed based on her review and synthesis of research on college access and choice, the proposed conceptual model has several assumptions. These assumptions build on the six central conclusions from the review of

FIGURE 2
Proposed Conceptual Model of Student Success

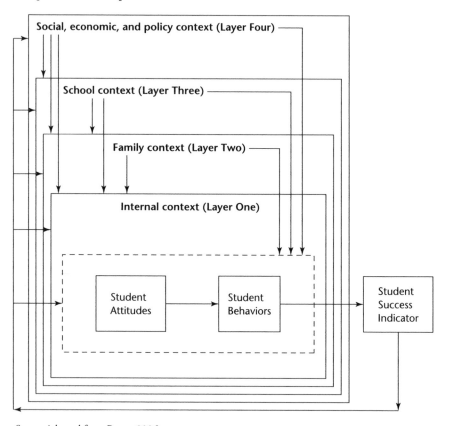

Source: Adapted from Perna, 2006a

disciplinary perspectives. Specifically, the model assumes that (1) the relative contribution of different disciplinary and area perspectives to student success varies; (2) when considered together, multiple theoretical approaches yield more comprehensive understandings of student success; (3) student success is shaped by multiple levels of context; (4) student success processes vary across groups; (5) multiple methodological approaches contribute to knowledge of student success; and (6) student success is a longitudinal process.

These assumptions underlie the multilayered conceptual model shown in Figure 2. As demonstrated in the previous section, relative attention to indicators of student success varies across disciplines. Thus, the proposed conceptual model assumes variation in the contribution of different disciplinary perspectives to knowledge of student success as well as to understanding the particular forces that shape student success.

Second, the model assumes that considering multiple perspectives together will yield new insights into the forces that promote and limit student success. The research review shows that, whereas articles published in top journals in psychology, sociology, and economics tend to rely only on perspectives that are derived from their particular discipline, a few articles in the top journals in education use conceptual models that draw on multiple theoretical perspectives. For example, several studies on college enrollment and choice illustrate the strengths of models that incorporate aspects of economic theories of human capital and sociological notions of cultural and social capital (for example, Freeman, 1997; Paulsen and St. John, 2002; Perna, 2000, 2004).

Other scholars recognize the benefits of drawing on multiple theoretical perspectives to examine college enrollment (see, for example, Perna, 2006a; St. John and Paulsen, 2001). Based on their review of the role of theory in finance-related analyses, St. John and Paulsen concluded that, "social and cultural theories are also important for the study of higher education finance because they provide an alternative, more complete explanation of the role of nonmonetary factors that foster and inhibit access" (2001, p. 555). Perna (2006a) concludes in her review of research on college student enrollment that no one perspective is sufficient for understanding differences across groups in two indicators of student success: college access and choice. Similarly, Manski (1993) demonstrates the strengths of a conceptual model (the Social Learning Proposition) that draws on constructs from both economics and sociology. He argues that economic approaches offer a framework for understanding decision making but are limited by their failure to examine the nature of information that is available to decision makers. On the other hand, sociological approaches shed light on the ways that individuals gather information but do not identify the ways that individuals make decisions based on this information (Manski, 1993). By considering multiple theoretical lenses together, research can address the limitations that are present in any one perspective.

Third, the conceptual model assumes that student success is influenced by multiple layers of context, including the internal context, the family context, the school context, and the broader social, economic, and political context. This assumption reflects the conclusion from the research review that, although the vast majority of research uses the student as the unit of analysis, research that uses multiple units of analysis may provide additional insights into the student success process. The research review also consistently shows that students make decisions and take actions that influence their success. But the decisions that students make and the behaviors in which they engage are shaped not only by the student's own characteristics but also by multiple levels of context (Perna, 2006a).

Because of its attention to multiple layers of context, the proposed model facilitates an examination of student success from different perspectives and different units of analysis. For policymakers and practitioners, the three most important units of analysis are students, the K–12 and higher education institutions they attend, and the public policies and programs that shape student and institutional behaviors. Incorporating different units of analysis is critical, given variations in each unit's definition of success. Clearly students have aims and objectives that are not always consistent with the goals and objectives of the institutions and policymakers that enable their education. Thus, students, institutions, and policymakers may evaluate success quite differently.

Fourth, by recognizing the role of multiple layers of context, the proposed conceptual model assumes that the path to student success is not universal but may vary across racial or ethnic, socioeconomic, and other groups based on differences in culture as well as differences in family resources, local school and community structures and supports, economic and social conditions, and public policies (Paulsen and St. John, 2002; Perna, 2006a; St. John and Asker, 2001). Although the degree of attention varies across disciplines, a substantial share of articles in top journals in all disciplines is concerned with variations across groups in student success processes. Like "the student choice construct" (Paulsen and St. John, 2002; St. John and Asker, 2001) and Perna's model (2006a) of college enrollment, the proposed model assumes that student success is determined, at least in part, by an individual's "situated context."

Because the situated context varies across individuals, multiple routes may lead to success (Perna, 2006a).

Fifth, consistent with the research review, the model also assumes that understandings of student success are informed by a variety of methodological approaches and sources of data. The proposed conceptual model recognizes the benefits of this diversity of methodological approaches and data sources and is intended to be tested using multiple methods. The proposed model allows for qualitative approaches that probe particular aspects of student success predictors, processes, or indicators as well as quantitative examinations of relationships among variables in or across particular layers of context.

Because of the explicit identification of the role of various layers of context, the model may also be productively used for studies that involve a range of sources of data, including single institution, state, and national samples. With the specification of layers of context, the proposed conceptual model provides a framework for organizing literature that involves varying sources of data.

Finally, the proposed model assumes that student success is a longitudinal process. Although disciplines vary in relative attention to particular student success indicators, consideration of multiple disciplines together shows the range of student success indicators that mark students' movement through the four student success transitions. Because researchers tend to examine discrete indicators of student success, however, examination of individual studies of student success obscures the extent to which success in one indicator contributes to success in other indicators.

Despite the absence of direct research, the proposed conceptual model assumes that student success is a longitudinal process that is marked by the four key transitions shown in Figure 1. In other words, the model assumes that student success is a process that begins with college readiness, moves on to college enrollment and then to college achievement, and culminates in postgraduate and labor market experiences. Figure 2 incorporates the longitudinal nature of the process through the use of feedback loops. The feedback loop (from the student success indicator back to the various layers of context) indicates that information about the attainment of any given student success indicator shapes the process for attaining other indicators of student success. In other words, the feedback loop indicates that a student's internal context—as well as the family, school, and policy context—are shaped in part by the attainment of other indicators of student success.

Conclusion

This chapter identifies and describes six conclusions that we drew from our review of articles published in "top" journals in each of four disciplines: economics, sociology, psychology, and education. Drawing on these six conclusions, the chapter proposes a multilayered conceptual model for understanding student success. The model assumes that the relative contribution of different disciplinary and area perspectives to student success varies; when considered together, multiple theoretical approaches yield more comprehensive understandings of student success; student success is shaped by multiple levels of context; student success processes vary across groups; multiple methodological approaches contribute to knowledge of student success; and student success is a longitudinal process. The four layers of context included in the proposed model are the internal context; the family context; the school context; and the broader social, economic and political context. The next chapter describes the disciplinary foundations of each of the four layers of the model.

Disciplinary Foundations of the Conceptual Model

DRAWING ON THE RESEARCH REVIEWED for this monograph, this chapter describes the disciplinary foundations for each of the four layers of the conceptual model. Given the parameters of the review (such as attention only to articles published in top journals in four disciplines), the substantive consideration of each layer is designed to be illustrative rather than comprehensive. In other words, the purpose of this discussion is not to provide an exhaustive assessment of the forces at all layers of context that contribute to all indicators of student success. Instead, this presentation illustrates the perspectives and emphases that each of the four disciplines contributes to each layer of the model. For each of the four layers of the model, we discuss research from the top journals in the following order: economics, sociology, psychology, and education.

Layer One: Internal Context

At its core, student success is determined by the attitudes, motivations, and behaviors of individual students. Our review suggests that, of the four disciplinary perspectives, psychology focuses greater attention than the other disciplines on understanding the cognitive and noncognitive processes that determine student success. Even the relatively small number of relevant articles in other disciplines and fields are centrally informed by psychological theories and frames. In short, psychology differs from the other disciplines included in this review in its decided focus on the individual's mental processes and behaviors—processes and behaviors defining Layer One of the model.

Economics

Aside from work only loosely coupled to cognitive dimensions of student success, the economics journals we reviewed yielded little insight into the contribution of Layer One to student success. An example of work loosely bearing on interests at this layer of the model is that of Jacob (2002), who models the influence of noncognitive skills on the gender gap in college participation. Jacob concludes that noncognitive skills influence college enrollment patterns even after controlling for high school performance and aptitude.

Sociology

Relatively little work published in top sociology journals examines cognitive or affective processes defining the internal context of success indicators. One notable exception, related to the work in psychology by Perry, Hladkyj, Pekrun, and Pelletier (2001), identifies the components of an academic work ethic among college students and shows how an academic work ethic is related to student performance and to characteristics of institutions attended (Rau and Durand, 2000). Rau and Durand conclude that a strong relationship exists between disciplined study, as defined by their academic ethic measure, and academic performance.

Psychology

Attention to the contribution of cognitive and noncognitive processes to student success is relatively common in psychology articles. More specifically, most of the articles published in top psychology journals inform understanding of the ways that such constructs as achievement motivation, self-efficacy, and stereotype threat contribute to student success.

A few articles published in top psychology journals focus on aspects of self-regulated learning, particularly perceived academic control and other strategies that regulate motivation. Research suggests that perceived academic control is positively related to final course grades and that students with high academic control and high preoccupation with failure receive the highest grades (Perry, Hladkyj, Pekrun, and Pelletier, 2001). Students with high academic control not only receive higher grades but also exert more effort, experience less anxiety, have greater motivation, tend to monitor progress in achieving goals, and perceive greater control over course assignments (Perry, Hladkyj, Pekrun, and Pelletier, 2001). Other research shows that students' strategies for regulating their motivation are related to their goal orientation (Wolters, 1998). The use of intrinsic regulation strategies is more common among those with mastery goal orientations, while use of extrinsic regulation strategies is more common among those with performance goal orientations (Wolters, 1998). High school students with autonomy orientations (that is, those who tend to participate in academic activities that they believe to be important to themselves) have more positive academic experiences, while students with control orientations (those who tend to participate in academic activities that they believe to be important to others) have lower academic performance and commitment (Wong, 2000).

A substantial number of articles published in top psychology journals examine the contribution of students' goals to their academic performance. This research consistently supports a "multiple goals" perspective, whereby mastery goals promote interest (Harackiewicz and others, 2000; Harackiewicz, Barron, Tauer, and Elliot, 2002), performance goals promote grades (Elliot and Church, 1997; Harackiewicz, Barron, Carter, and Lehto, 1997; Harackiewicz and others, 2000; Harackiewicz, Barron, Tauer, and Elliot, 2002), and performance avoidance goals reduce academic performance (Elliot and Church, 1997). The positive relationship between performance goals and academic achievement appears to be mediated by such variables as persistence on task (Elliot, McGregor, and Gable, 1999); effort, self-efficacy, goal level (VandeWalle, Cron, and Slocum, 2001); and achievement motivation (Barron and Harackiewicz, 2001), while the negative relationship between performance avoidance goals and academic achievement appears to be mediated by test anxiety (Elliot and McGregor, 1999) and disorganization (Elliot, McGregor, and Gable, 1999).

Research published in top psychology journals consistently shows that academic self-efficacy, optimism, and hope are positively related to students' academic performance (Brackney and Karabenick, 1995; Chemers, Hu, and Garcia, 2001; Gibbons and others, 2000; Snyder and others, 2002). The effects of such "trait-like" characteristics as general self-efficacy, goal orientation, and cognitive ability on academic achievement may be mediated by such "state-like" characteristics as task-specific self-efficacy (Chen, Gully, Whiteman, and

Kilcullen, 2000). Psychopathology (psychological disorders, including anxiety and substance abuse disorders) is negatively related to students' academic performance directly (Svanum and Zody, 2001) and indirectly through self-efficacy and resource management (Brackney and Karabenick, 1995).

With only a few exceptions (for example, Cullen, Hardison, and Sackett, 2004), research in top psychology journals consistently shows that stereotype threat contributes to gaps in academic performance between blacks and whites (Brown and others, 2000; Gonzales, Blanton, and Williams, 2002; Steele and Aronson, 1995), women and men (Brown and others, 2000; Brown and Josephs, 1999; Gonzales, Blanton, and Williams, 2002; O'Brien and Crandall, 2003), and students with and without mental illness (Quinn, Kahng, and Crocker, 2004). A self-evaluative stereotype threat is assumed to negatively influence performance when an individual's focus is diverted from performing a particular task to worrying that low performance will confirm a negative stereotype about a group to which the individual belongs (Steele and Aronson, 1995). The negative effects of stereotype threat on performance may be reduced by other psychological characteristics, particularly a coping sense of humor (Ford, Ferguson, Brooks, and Hagadone, 2004).

Other research in top psychology journals shows the negative effects of particular experiences for African Americans. A longitudinal study of African Americans at one predominantly white institution showed that grades declined over the period of the study for students who had high levels of race-related rejection sensitivity (those who "anxiously expect, readily perceive, and intensely react to rejection in situations where rejection is possible" (Mendoza-Denton and others, 2002, p. 896). Other research suggests that, compared with other African American high school students, those who had positive feelings about their racial group and viewed race as important to their identity had higher rates of college enrollment, while those who felt few connections to their racial group and had negative beliefs about their racial group had lower rates of college enrollment (Chavous and others, 2003).

Articles in psychology journals also include attention to differences in academic performance between women and men, describing gender differences in rates of Advanced Placement test taking and performance (Stumpf and Stanley, 1996) and explaining that gender differences in SAT math scores are attributable in part to gender differences in mental rotation ability and math self-confidence (Casey, Nuttall, Pezaris, and Benbow, 1995; Casey, Nuttall, and Pezaris, 1997). Other research shows gender differences in the relationship between psychopathology and semester grades (Svanum and Zody, 2001), between control orientation and academic experiences (Wong, 2000), and between text anxiety and grade point average (Chapell and others, 2005).

A small number of articles published in top psychology journals suggest links between the internal layer of context and the school context (that is, Layer Two of the model) via students' perceptions of this context. For example, one study suggests that increased perceptions of "situational constraints" (quantity and quality of resources available to support learning) indirectly reduce academic performance by reducing students' performance goals (Villanova, 1996). A second study shows that undergraduates' academic achievement is positively related to students' beliefs about school, particularly their predisposition toward the learning context (Larose and Roy, 1995).

Education

Only a small number of articles in top education journals examine the ways that students' cognitive and noncognitive skills shape their success. Moreover, the education articles that include this focus tend to draw on psychological constructs. For example, one article shows that students' academic performance in college is shaped by cognitive skills (as measured by test scores) as well as by noncognitive variables, including motivation and use of self-regulated learning strategies (Ruban and McCoach, 2005). Other work stresses the contribution of self-efficacy to students' academic achievement. In a review and synthesis of prior research, Pajares (1996) concludes that self-efficacy beliefs shape student effort and perseverance, which in turn influence subsequent academic performance. In other educational research, performance is viewed as a function of self-worth beliefs related to mathematics and gender (Stage and Kloosterman, 1995).

Summary

The proposed conceptual model assumes that, at the "core" (Layer One of the model), student success is determined by an individual's motivations and attitudes. Our examination of research published in the top journals in each of four disciplines shows the dominance of psychological perspectives for understanding these core attributes.

Layer Two: Family Context

The second layer of the model, the family context, recognizes that both inside and outside the home, families may "manage" their children's experiences to promote various indicators of student success (Furstenberg and others, 1999; McDonough, 1997; Perna and Titus, 2005). Although the aspect of families that is emphasized varies across disciplines, research using each of the four disciplinary perspectives includes attention to the influence of families on student success.

Economics

Our research review identified several examples of the ways that economists view the contribution of families to student success. Some research in top economics journals examines the role of parents' occupation. One study shows that, compared with peers with traditionally employed parents, young people from families with family-owned businesses generally have lower academic performance during high school and are less likely to enroll in college (Davila and Mora, 2004). Ease of intergenerational transfer of these family-owned businesses is presumed to discourage academic engagement in high school and diminish college-going aspirations of children in these entrepreneurial families (Davila and Mora, 2004). In other work addressing the occupational background of families, Siegfried and Getz (2006) develop a novel analysis of college choice patterns of students from families with at least one parent who works on a university faculty. Siegfried and Getz were particularly interested in the degree to which these students may be advantaged by additional information about college quality that would be transmitted by their more knowledgeable parent(s). Although failing to provide a causal explanation, Siegfried and Getz note that students in their sample are more likely to attend research universities and selective liberal arts colleges than are their peers from nonacademic families.

Economists have also examined the contribution of family structure to student success. For example, Ver Ploeg (2002) isolated the effects of displaced children on the likelihood of college enrollment and degree attainment. Although previous researchers have explained this disadvantage as a function of the typically diminished income of broken homes, Ver Ploeg controls for income and reveals a net negative effect of such circumstance.

Beyond the structural characteristics of families, economists have also devoted attention to dimensions such as the economic behavior of families with children in college. One example of this perspective is Bodvarsson and Walker (2004), who find that students whose parents pay for a substantial proportion of the costs associated with tuition and living expenses have lower grade point averages, are more likely to fail courses, and are less likely to persist to the baccalaureate than students who bear the lion's share of these costs themselves through work or personal savings.

Sociology

Sociologists have made a number of important contributions to our understanding of the influence of family characteristics on student success. Cheng and Starks (2002) employ a symbolic interaction frame to examine the differential role of significant others on the educational expectations of students from different racial groups. Symbolic interaction focuses on the ways that personal identity is developed through the interaction with others. The Cheng and Starks work points to processes through which the influences of significant others are conditioned by race. Central to their findings is the idea that the power of specific significant others (such as parents, teachers, or friends) to influence expectations about education varies across racial groups.

Some research shows the role that families play in determining the future paths of their children and ultimately the degree to which those future paths may reduce or magnify stratification in broader society. Conley's account (2001) of the role of family wealth in college attendance and completion shows that traditional models of attainment have ignored the role of family wealth, focusing instead on less useful measures of family income. This type of analysis taps a long-standing sociological interest in the long-term advantages conveyed through the intergenerational transfer of wealth. Other sociological research focuses on families and high schools and the ways that family background can determine students' preparation for college and range of choices available. For example,

---

Attewell (2001) argues that families seek to maximize the quality of schooling available to their children, often with the hope of improving their chances for college success. He shows that this pursuit on the part of the family may actually be counterproductive in terms of chances for admission to high-quality colleges. Other research shows that family background has an important influence on high school performance and college enrollment (see, for example, Muller and Schiller, 2000; Conley, 2001; Crosnoe, 2001; Cheng and Starks, 2002; Karen, 2002; Hofferth, Boisjoly, and Duncan, 1998). This influence is channeled through increased parental involvement (Crosnoe, 2001), noneconomic (cultural) by-products of family wealth (Conley, 2001), the influence of significant others (Cheng and Starks, 2002), and the social networks and cultural connections of parents (Hofferth, Boisjoly, and Duncan, 1998).

Most of the sociological literature is dominated by either an exclusive cultural reproduction framing or some type of contrast between the reproduction models and mobility models. Although reproduction models place primacy on the binding role of social origins, mobility models focus on the degree to which social status can change over the course of a lifetime. Education is a central feature in both models, serving as a reproductive mechanism in the former and a democratizing mechanism in the latter. A notable example of such a contrast is Aschaffenburg and Maas's examination (1997) of the role of cultural capital in school success. In that work they test competing mobility (DiMaggio, 1982) and reproduction theories (Bourdieu and Passeron, 1977) and conclude that the mobility model is dominant but that the reproduction model is the more important in terms of college enrollment.

Psychology

A number of articles in top psychology journals examine the influence of the family context on student success. Among the relevant aspects of the family context, from the perspective of this discipline, are strength of ties to parents, parenting style, and parents' job security. The sole qualitative psychological article in this review suggests that students' plans are shaped, at least in part, by the tension between increasing autonomy and sustaining ties to parents and other loved ones (Shilkret and Nigrosh, 1997). Other research shows that students' academic achievement is influenced by parenting style, although the relationship appears to be weaker for college seniors than for other students (Glasgow and others, 1997; Strage and Brandt, 1999). An exploratory study suggests that, when students perceive job insecurity among their parents, the students experience cognitive problems, which reduce students' academic performance (Barling, Zacharatos, and Hepburn, 1999).

Other research published in top psychology journals shows that the relationship between aspects of the family context and student success varies based on parents' educational attainment, ethnicity, and immigrant status. Research shows variations based on parents' educational attainment and ethnicity in the effects of parental involvement on eleventh grade students' educational and occupational aspirations (Hill and others, 2004) and students' academic achievement (Hong and Ho, 2005). Other research shows that, compared with students from United States-born families, students from immigrant families have higher academic motivation (which promotes academic achievement) but greater family demands (which reduce academic achievement [Tseng, 2004]).

Education

A substantial share of articles in education show that student success is related to students' sociodemographic characteristics, particularly socioeconomic status, race, and ethnicity. Educational research consistently shows that, even after taking into account other variables, socioeconomic status is positively associated with such measures of student success as choice of institution attended (Astin and Oseguera, 2004; Perna and Titus, 2004; Teranishi and others, 2004) and graduate school enrollment (Walpole, 2003; Zhang, 2005a). Educational research also shows that the predictors of such indicators as predisposition to college (Hamrick and Stage, 1998), college enrollment (Heller, 1999), college grade point average (Hoffman and Lowitzki, 2005), and plans for graduate school (Pascarella, Wolniak, Flowers, and Pierson, 2004) vary by racial/ethnic group. Although fewer studies examine variations in broad racial or ethnic categories, the small amount of available research shows that such indicators as choice of institution attended vary by ethnicity in a particular group (for example, Asian Pacific American [Teranishi and others, 2004]).

Research in education also includes attention to the role of family or parental involvement in promoting student success. In particular, articles in top educational journals have examined the contribution of parental involvement to such indicators as college enrollment (Perna, 2000; Perna and Titus, 2005) and the role of family background in shaping impressions and realities of attendance and choice constraints (Paulsen and St. John, 2002).

Summary

All four disciplinary perspectives inform our understanding of the ways that the family context (Layer Two of the model) influences student success. Economists have examined the influence on student success of such characteristics as parents' occupation and family structure as well as parents' role in paying college prices. For sociologists, families are central to "status attainment" frameworks and perspectives examining the sources of continued stratification of educational opportunity and outcomes. Psychologists include attention to the strength of ties to parents, parenting style, and parents' job security as well as variations in outcomes based on family characteristics. Educational researchers often examine the contribution to student success of such characteristics as socioeconomic status and parents' involvement in their children's education.

Layer Three: School Context

Layer Three of the model, the school context, reflects the attention that various disciplines, particularly economics, sociology, and education, devote to understanding the contribution of K-12 schools and higher education institutions to student success. Attention to the school context, from primary school through college, enables the identification and understanding of compounding effects that determine the educational resources, academic preparation, and educational orientations that subsequently determine success at the college level.

Economics

School effects are an important domain of study in economics. Much of the economics literature in this layer addresses the role of years, type, and quality of education on subsequent indicators of student success. A review of literature published in top economics journals suggests three themes pertaining to the relationship between institutional characteristics and practices and student success indicators: (1) interplay between two-year and four-year institutions; (2) economic returns to institutional characteristics; and (3) the effects of institutional packaging of financial aid on retention and degree attainment.

Economists have devoted significant attention to understanding differences between and relationships among influences of two- and four-year institutions. The subbaccalaureate labor market is the focus of Grubb (2002a, 2002b), who, through reviews and his own empirical analysis, concludes that, although there is little effect of course taking by itself, there exists a significant return to completion of subbaccalaureate credentials in certain areas. Alfonso, Bailey, and Scott (2005), however, show that "occupationally" oriented students are less likely to complete their degree programs and call attention to mission ambiguity in today's community colleges. Other researchers focus on the difference in returns among two- and four-year graduates (see, for example, Kane and Rouse, 1995), concluding that, relative to high school graduates, an earnings premium exists at each level of attainment and to a lesser degree for those leaving college without a degree (Grubb, 2002a; U.S. Census Bureau, 2004).

The role of the two-year school in determining aspirations, transfer behavior, and completion has been the focus of a number of researchers in the economics literature. Ehrenberg and Smith (2004) develop a useful evaluation scheme for states to use in determining the degree to which four-year institutions graduate two-year transfer students. Their framework calls attention to the role the two-year schools play in terms of academic preparation and the responsiveness of four-year institutions to the needs of these transfers. Leigh and Gill (2003, 2004) show how two-year schools enhance educational aspirations of their graduates and improve their probabilities of baccalaureate attainment. Taken together, Sandy, Gonzalez, and Hilmer (2006) and Gonzalez and Hilmer (2006) show that two-year colleges democratize opportunity and improve the likelihood of baccalaureate attainment for Hispanic students in particular. They explain the lower rates of baccalaureate attainment by two-year transfers as a function of their propensity to transfer to lower-quality four-year institutions rather than inadequate preparation at the two-year level (Gonzales and Hilmer, 2006). Surette (2001) focuses on gender differences in two- to four-year transfer, failing to arrive at a plausible explanation for the persistently lower rate of transfer and completion among women than men.

While Kane and Rouse (1995) focus on two- and four-year rates of return, Arias and McMahon (2001) focus on an improved model for estimating private rates of return (which they claim have been seriously underestimated in most of the economics literature). Looking beyond direct wage benefits, Eide (Eide and Waehrer, 1998; Eide, Brewer, and Ehrenberg, 1998) offers considerations of the option value that more selective colleges confer on their graduates and argues that a sole focus on wage premiums obscures the larger picture of benefits accruing to graduates from more prestigious schools.

Pricing and the influence of financial constraints in attendance decisions and college choices have also received a great deal of attention in the economics literature. For example, financial constraint has been shown to play a lesser role in college choice at the application stage than students' sense of institutional fit (Toutkoushian, 2001). Analyzing college application behavior, Toutkoushian concludes that a student's sense of ability relative to that of the student body at colleges in a potential choice pool plays a larger role in deciding where to apply than does their sense of affordability.

Although substantial work has been devoted to understanding the effects of financial aid and subsidies on student attendance patterns more broadly, the literature at Layer Three reveals economists' interest in institutional behaviors relating to aid and subsidies that can influence student attendance. Good examples of research along this line include Singell (2004) and Kerkvliet and Nowell (2005). Both studies examine the role of aid in persistence and arrive at different but not conflicting conclusions: aid matters but it depends on the context of the institution and degree to which students are influenced by their perceptions of opportunity costs.

Sociology

Sociologists also devote substantial attention to the role of the school context, with particular focus on structural antecedents to postsecondary student success indicators. Much of the research that is relevant to this layer focuses on theoretical tensions between cultural reproduction and social mobility. Karen (2002) paints a powerful picture of stratified opportunity, showing that although disadvantaged students begin with a lower chance of college continuation, those that do go on most often enroll in less selective institutions that provide fewer academic support resources—institutions that have also been shown to confer lesser returns in the postgraduation labor market (Thomas 2000; Thomas and Zhang, 2005).

The process through which students are advantaged as a result of their K-12 experiences is an important interest of sociologists. Attewell (2001) and Espenshade, Hale, and Chung (2005) have scrutinized the effects of the ultra-competitive high school environments that many parents seek for their children. Attewell's analysis (also cited in our consideration at Layer Two of the model) suggests that these schools penalize students because of the probability of an otherwise top-performing student's being ranked lower in the class simply because of the intense academic competition. Espenshade, Hale, and Chung (2005) revised this "frog-pond" effect and reaffirmed Attewell's findings with the important qualification that the overall performance of students in the schools generally outweighs any disadvantage resulting from lower ranking as a result of the intensity of competition at the school.

Alon and Tienda (2005) and Hurtado and Carter (1997) address issues of institutional "fit" among minority and Latino students, respectively. Alon and Tienda (2005) develop a more nuanced model to estimate the success rates of minority students attending highly selective institutions, concluding that, when modeled properly, the rates of minority and nonminority student success at these institutions is the same. In contrast, Hurtado and Carter (1997) find that Latino students' sense of belonging on four-year campuses after transfer from a two-year school is not as strong as for their peers who enrolled as native freshmen on the four-year campus.

Although the majority of work in sociology addresses issues related to the process by which schools structure opportunities for success at the postsecondary level, a few studies examine program effectiveness in colleges. Two studies of interest have already been cited as examples of work addressing issues in Layer One of our model. The first of them is Rau and Durand's examination (2000) of the academic work ethic and its relationship to academic performance. Although the idea of an ethic clearly relates to Layer One, the study also provides insight about how colleges could best foster this ethic on their campuses. Collier (2000) was concerned with the impact of capstone course experiences on the development of student identity, which is in turn linked to academic performance. Similar to Rau and Durand, Collier offers a consideration of what colleges might be able to do to make these programs effective on their campuses. Additional sociological work on program effects includes Deil-Amen and Rosenbaum's examination (2002) of "stigma free" remediation programs at two-year colleges. They use a qualitative approach and conclude that the "stigma free" programs can work, sometimes too well. They note that some students failed to develop a realistic sense of their abilities and therefore held unrealistic expectations about their future academic opportunities. Regina and James (2004) examine differences between two-year for-profit and not-for-profit schools' programs for maximizing employment possibilities for their graduates. They conclude that community colleges could benefit from institutionalizing their employment processes in ways that are similar to their for-profit counterparts.

Psychology

Only a small number of articles in top psychology journals examine the influence of school context on student success, suggesting that psychology theories may be less relevant than other perspectives to understanding this layer. The available psychology articles generally illustrate the ways that particular interventions or experiences contribute to various aspects of student success. For example, one study shows that the negative effects of stereotype threat on female students' math performance are reduced when students learn of a "disconfirming example," for example, a female role model in math performance (Marx and Roman, 2002). Another study shows that, by building interpersonal skills and educational aspirations, participating in extracurricular activities contributes to higher levels of educational attainment at age 20 (Mahoney, Cairns, and Farmer, 2003). A third study shows that students who request and receive personal psychological counseling have higher retention rates than students who request but do not receive counseling (Wilson, Mason, and Ewing, 1997). Another study suggests that, among students with high levels of emotional and psychological stress, an intervention that requires students to write about the stress prevents a decline in grade point average (Lumley and Provenzano, 2003). Providing students with a decision-making aid that helps them to identify the reasons for their decision improves students' satisfaction with their choice of college (Kmett, Arkes, and Jones, 1999). Other research suggests that students' SAT verbal scores (but not course grades) depend in part on their relative skill with multiple-choice rather than essay examinations (Bridgeman and Morgan, 1996).

Education

Educational research also recognizes the role of the institutional context in determining student success. Some studies demonstrate that particular indicators of student success are associated with the characteristics of the high school attended, while other indicators are related to the characteristics of the higher education institution. For example, studies show that high school context is directly related to college access and choice. Factors such as high school quality and ethnic mix shape students' opportunity for college; these high school influences are known to vary by racial background (Perna, 2000). Other work shows that choosing to attend a historically black college or university rather than a predominantly white institution is related, at least in part, to the characteristics of the high school attended and students' experiences at that school (Freeman, 1999). High schools with well-developed guidance and advising programs have also been shown to have important influences on subsequent college enrollment behaviors and institutional choices (Plank and Jordan, 2001; Tierney and Jun, 2001).

In terms of the higher education context, research in top educational journals shows that such institutional characteristics as single sex, race, and quality contribute to student success. Based on his review of research, Mael (1998) concludes that academic achievement is higher for students who attend a single-sex institution (junior high school, high school, or college) rather than a coeducational institution. Other research suggests that success varies in part based on whether a student attends a historically black college or university or a predominantly white institution, with black students having more positive experiences at historically black colleges or universities than at predominantly white institutions (Fleming, 2002; Fries-Britt and Turner, 2002). The quality of the higher education institution attended is positively related to such indicators of student success as graduate school enrollment and degree completion as well as earnings (Zhang, 2005a, 2005b), and institutional expenditure patterns are related to students' self-reported gains in various aspects of college performance (Toutkoushian and Smart, 2001).

Other educational research focuses on the contribution to student success indicators of particular programs or experiences at an institution. Using an experimental design, Nagda and others (1998) found that participation in an undergraduate research opportunity increased rates of persistence through graduation, especially for African Americans with academic achievement below the median. Other research suggests that participating in community service is positively related to such indicators as graduate school enrollment and degree attainment (Astin, Sax, and Avalos, 1999). Reviews of research suggest that academic achievement improves when a student participates in some form of peer assessment (Topping, 1998) or participates in an intervention designed to enhance study skills (Hattie, Biggs, and Purdie, 1996). For science, mathematics, engineering, and technology courses and programs, academic achievement and persistence increase when the student engages in some form of small-group learning (Springer, Stanne, and Donovan, 1999).

Summary

The conceptual model also assumes that context of the "school" attended, including both K-12 and higher education institutions, influences student success. Attention to the school context is relatively more common in economics, sociology, and education than in psychology. Economic frameworks may be particularly useful for informing our understanding of differences in outcomes for students attending two-year and four-year colleges and universities, the economic returns to different characteristics of colleges and universities, and the effects of a college or university's financial aid programs on student outcomes. Sociological perspectives shed light on the ways that K-12 schools and higher education institutions structure educational opportunities for students. Drawing on both economic and sociological perspectives, education research also stresses the ways that school and college characteristics influence various indicators of student success. Psychological perspectives may be especially useful for understanding how the effects of a particular policy or program on a given outcome may be mediated by cognitive and affective processes.

Layer Four: Social, Economic, and Policy Context

The fourth layer of the model, the social, economic, and policy context, recognizes that numerous external forces also influence student college choice, both directly and indirectly through other layers of context (Perna, 2006a). Although less commonly examined than the other layers of the model, at least some research in all four disciplines suggests the importance of considering how the social, economic, and policy context influences student success. Among the potentially influential forces are social conditions (societal norms), economic conditions (unemployment rate), and public policies (establishment of a new state-sponsored non-need-based grant program).

Economics

Economists have contributed significantly to our understanding of issues connected to this layer of the model. Representative work addresses the role that state aid policies play in college choice (Niu, Tienda, and Cortes, 2006) and the ways that education-related debt influences employment decisions (Minicozzi, 2005) and educational attainment (Monks, 2001). Supply and demand issues related to regulation and state appropriations for higher education present challenges for state struggles to maintain enrollment levels (Berger and Kostal, 2002). As demand inevitably declines when tuition increases, Berger and Kostal (2002) argue that states must choose between reducing supply through further reductions in appropriations or increasing regulation of colleges and universities. Supply and demand are dominant themes in work related to this layer. Additional research in this layer of our proposed conceptual model considers effects of public financing of K-12 schools (Deke, 2003) and the role of financial aid (Dynarski, 2002; Keane, 2002; Ichimura and Taber, 2002).

Sociology

Sociological inquiry draws attention to the ways that larger societal inequities may be related to higher education. Some of this work focuses on occupational gender segregation and its relationship to persistent gender bias in students' choice of major (Bradley, 2000). Other work in sociology attempts to account for observed increases in women's participation in science and engineering major fields. For example, Ramirez and Wotipka (2001) suggest that increased participation in science and engineering fields is simply a function of increased participation overall by women. More refined analyses of gender bias in occupations and earnings conclude that women's major choices limit their occupational choices and that

---

women are more likely to find themselves in lower-paying government and non-profit jobs (Roksa, 2005). Roksa's work also shows that, despite lower pay in these jobs, women tend to enjoy more rapid elevation to management positions.

Psychology

Very few articles published in top psychology journals inform understanding of the contribution of the social, economic, and policy context to student success. One exception shows the role of the media in shaping student success. This study suggests that, by activating stereotype threat, stereotypic commercials contribute to lower math performance among women than men (Davies, Spencer, Quinn, and Gerhardstein, 2002).

Education

A small number of articles in educational journals illustrate the role of the policy context in shaping student success. Some research shows that aspects of such state public policies as tuition, financial aid, appropriations, and K-12 academic preparation are related to college access and choice (Heller, 1997, 1999; Perna and Titus, 2004), while other research shows that racial or ethnic stratification in college enrollment increased in one state despite the presence of various higher education policies (Perna, Steele, Woda, and Hibbert, 2005). K-12 educational reform, challenges to affirmative action, and changed student demographics appear to shape college admissions processes (Sireci, Zanetti, and Berger, 2003). Although desegregation initiatives are typically associated with increased enrollment of black students in predominantly white colleges, one study shows that desegregation initiatives and demographic changes appear to have contributed to greater enrollment of white than black students at one historically black college (Brown, 2002).

Summary

The outermost layer of the model explicitly recognizes that aspects of the social, economic, and policy context may also shape student success. Economic perspectives appear particularly useful for informing our understanding of the ways that particular public policies influence student success. Sociological perspectives draw attention to the role of broad social forces and social inequities. Although few articles in psychology journals appear relevant to this layer (that is, Layer Four of the model), one potentially relevant perspective considers the role of the media in shaping student success. By including attention to federal and state public policies, demographic changes, and other forces, education research also suggests that the social, economic, and policy context influences student success.

Conclusion

This chapter illustrates the perspectives that four disciplines (economics, sociology, psychology, and education) contribute to each of the four layers of the conceptual model. The chapter also offers examples of studies from each of the four disciplines for each layer of the model. Based on our review of research published in top journals, we conclude that psychological perspectives dominate the understanding of the "internal context" of student success (Layer One of the model). With their focus on an individual's cognitive and affective processes, psychological perspectives seem ideally suited for understanding how such core attributes as an individual's attitudes and motivations influence student success. Although stressing different facets, all four disciplinary perspectives recognize the contribution of the family context (Layer Two of the model) to student success. Economics, sociology, and education perspectives often include attention to the ways that characteristics of the K-12 schools and higher education institutions that students attend (Layer Three of the model) influence student success, while psychological perspectives typically devote less attention to this layer of context. A review of research in these four disciplines also sheds light on the various ways that student success is influenced by the broader social, economic, and policy context (Layer Four). The final chapter builds on these understandings to offer implications of the model for policymakers and practitioners as well as future researchers.

Implications of the Proposed Conceptual Model

THE PERSISTENCE OF SOCIOECONOMIC, racial or ethnic, and gender gaps in many dimensions of success suggests that traditional approaches to understanding sources of such gaps are insufficient. Rather than identifying a panacea for raising student success for all students and reducing student success gaps among students, the proposed conceptual model offers a framework for policymakers and practitioners who are interested in working toward these goals. The proposed conceptual framework offers a guide to the development, implementation, and evaluation of policies and practices related to student success. Although existing policies, practices, and research generally focus on discrete aspects of student success, the proposed conceptual model encourages policymakers, practitioners, and researchers to view any student success intervention or indicator as part of a broader and longitudinal student success process. The proposed conceptual model also assumes that incorporating and drawing on multiple theoretical and methodological approaches results in a more complete understanding of the complexity of student success processes and indicators.

This chapter first identifies implications of the proposed model for policymakers and practitioners who are interested in identifying ways to improve student success. The chapter then offers recommendations for how the proposed conceptual model may be used to guide future research on student success.

Implications for Policymakers and Practitioners

The proposed conceptual model offers at least four suggestions for policymakers and practitioners who seek to improve success for all students and reduce gaps in success among students. The suggestions offer guidance for the development and implementation of policy and practice.

First, policymakers and practitioners should recognize that policies and practices are enacted through multiple layers of context. Therefore, to reduce gaps in student success across groups, policymakers and practitioners should recognize the limitations on student success that may be imposed by a student's situated context. Clearly, the effectiveness of policies and practices depends on ways that these policies and practices are interpreted and enacted as well as the transmission of policies and practices through various levels of context. Policymakers and practitioners should recognize that the effectiveness of a particular policy or practice cannot be assessed merely in terms of the availability of a program or policy to a student but also in terms of the layers of context that inform the student's understanding of the program or policy and that encourage or limit participation of the students in the policy or program. In other words, as reflected by the conceptual model, policymakers and practitioners should recognize the tension between the roles of student agency and structure, that is, the ways that the broader structure of social and educational opportunities shapes the range of options students view as realistic.

As an example, the federal government supports the student financial aid programs authorized by the Higher Education Act in an effort to increase student access to college (one indicator of student success). The effectiveness of these federal programs in accomplishing this goal, however, depends on the ways that the programs are enacted through various levels of context. Students' use of federal financial aid is likely shaped not only by the availability of the aid but also by the extent to which higher education institutions and schools provide information to the student about the availability of the aid (Layer Three in Figure 2) (Perna, 2006b). Students' use of federal financial aid is also likely shaped by the extent to which students and their families are able to gain access to information about financial aid (Layers One and Two) and the extent to which students define college as a realistic option (Layer One) (Perna, 2006b).

Second, policymakers and practitioners should develop and implement policies in ways that recognize that policies and programs do not operate in isolation but interact with other policies and programs and with characteristics of the schools, families, and students. Federal and state policymakers as well as K-12 and higher education leaders have developed numerous policies and programs that are all designed to address a particular aspect of student success. Typically policies and programs are developed individually, with little coordination among policies and programs. In addition, individual policies and programs are typically designed to address discrete indicators of student success.

A good example of the lack of coordination among policies with similar goals can be found in the efforts made by some states to require students to pass a "high-stakes" examination as a requirement for high school graduation. Four-year colleges and universities typically require students to take a different test such as the SAT or ACT as a requirement for admission. The structure and content of the high school exit exams and college entrance exams are typically developed in isolation. Both tests are designed to promote academic preparation and assess academic achievement, but the lack of alignment or coordination of policies surrounding use of these exams means that students graduate from high school under a set of expectations that may be needlessly disconnected from the realities that a majority of graduates will experience upon entering the college classroom–a disconnect that may in part explain the heavy subscription to remedial courses during the first year of college (Kirst and Venezia, 2004).

Third, policymakers and practitioners should also recognize that, because multiple layers of context inform student success, no single approach to policy or practice will improve student success for all students or reduce gaps in success across students. Policies and programs that recognize variations in the various layers of context are likely to be more effective than policies and programs that emphasize a one-size-fits-all approach.

As an example, research suggests that financial aid promotes college access and choice for many students, but particular forms of financial aid, especially loans, are less effective in promoting college enrollment and choice for some groups of students than for others. Willingness to borrow varies based on the characteristics of the school attended, with students attending high schools with higher levels of student achievement and socioeconomic status generally being willing to borrow and students attending high schools with lower levels of student achievement and socioeconomic status being less willing (Perna, in press). Differences in use of loans to finance college costs appears to have contributed to lower enrollment rates for Hispanics and American Indians than for whites (ECMC Group Foundation, 2003). African Americans, American Indians, and Hispanics are more likely than whites to enroll in lower-cost postsecondary educational institutions without borrowing even after controlling for socioeconomic characteristics (ECMC Group Foundation, 2003).

Finally, policymakers and practitioners should support a program of research that tests aspects of the conceptual model using multiple methods and drawing on multiple theoretical perspectives. Despite the large number of studies that examine various aspects of student success, our review of research identified few studies that used multiple units of analysis or multiple theoretical perspectives. In addition, few articles included attention to understanding the contribution of multiple layers of context to the effectiveness of policies and programs.

Implications for Researchers

This monograph demonstrates that knowledge of student success has been shaped by scholars in a range of disciplines. In many ways this scholarship has been motivated by disciplinary interests in the psychological, social, and economic behaviors of students. Indeed, much of the research in these disciplines that we reviewed for this monograph focuses on student success indicators primarily as a means to test theories about broader relationships that occupy the attention of scholars in a particular field, with no more than a secondary interest in identifying practical ways to improve student success.

Therefore, although a rich corpus of research on student success exists, this body of research has largely evolved in the context of specific disciplines that are interested in a much wider range of problems and that use constructs that are less concrete than those that would readily promote a theory of student success or even a more policy-relevant understanding of student success indicators. Consider, for example, the varied ways that scholars in different fields approach the issue of student persistence. Economists emphasize the roles of cost and benefits, price response, credit constraints, and labor market opportunities in shaping persistence behavior. Sociologists emphasize the relationship between ties to specific student reference groups and persistence and variations in these relationships by race, class, and gender. Psychologists emphasize individual achievement motivation, self-efficacy, and the cognitive dimensions of academic performance that are presumed to inform persistence behavior. Each of these three perspectives approaches a specific student success outcome (such as persistence) as a vehicle for better understanding concepts that are central to the particular discipline.

To provide the empirical foundation for developing policies and programs that promote student success, academic researchers must bridge the disconnect between their approaches and the needs of policymakers. Given the range of disciplinary approaches that are used and the applied nature of the research, researchers in the field of education are especially well positioned to lead efforts that not only reflect the orientations of academic scholars but also address the need of policymakers to identify practical ways to effectively improve student success.

This monograph offers a conceptual framework for guiding a systematic program of research on student success. Future research should examine the usefulness of the model for (1) bridging research and policy, (2) incorporating insights from a range of methodological approaches and sources of data, (3) understanding other indicators of student success, and (4) developing multi- and interdisciplinary approaches to understanding student success.

First, a primary purpose of future research should be to test the extent to which the proposed conceptual model may be used to develop and implement policies and practices that more effectively promote success for all students and reduce success gaps among students. Although the conceptual model presented in this monograph was developed based on a review and synthesis of research, the model has yet to be tested empirically. Research is required to test the relationships outlined in this model and to more fully specify the relationships that operate in particular aspects of the model. Research should include explicit attention to particular aspects of the model, including the contribution of aspects of each layer to student success and interactions in and between layers. For example, research should examine the ways that multiple institutional policies and practices (remediation, financial aid, and advising) together and individually promote particular aspects of student success. As a second example, research should also examine the ways that federal financial aid policies (Layer Four) are enacted by institutions (Layer Three) to shape students' aspirations, enrollment, performance, and degree attainment (Layer One).

Second, future research should test the relationships identified in the proposed conceptual model using a range of methodological approaches and sources of data. The small share of qualitative studies identified in our research review should not be interpreted as a conclusion about the relative contributions of this method for understanding student success and the processes that link predictors of student success to various indicators of student success in particular contexts. Although qualitative research is often viewed as descriptive under the humanist or postmodernist traditions, this view neglects the long and critical evolution of qualitative inquiry and its role in the development of theory. In short, the inductive dimension of theory development "fundamentally depends on watching people in their own territory and interacting with them in their own language" (Kirk and Miller, 1986, p. 9). Less concerned with generalization to a particular population, qualitative approaches are inherently valuable in situating relationships in native and often essential contexts. Used together to connect the inductive-deductive chain that informs good research, both qualitative and quantitative approaches will enhance our understanding of student success.

Qualitative inquiry may be effectively used, for example, to gain insight into the ways that families with different cultural backgrounds promote college opportunity for their children. Although exhaustive inventorying and detailing of the policies and programs aimed at encouraging college going can provide an accurate accounting of the programs that policymakers have put in place, the examination of such data does not capture the situated context in which students and their families view, understand, and use these programs. Qualitative research can serve as a powerful vehicle for understanding the field of forces that shapes intended users' understandings of policies that are often created at a great distance from the location at which an influence is sought.

Third, future research in education should test the conceptual model using a broader range of student success indicators. The literature review for this monograph was limited to studies that examined a narrow set of indicators of student success. Nonetheless, attention to a wider range of indicators would likely enhance our understanding of processes that contribute to raising success for all students and reducing gaps in success among students. Future research should test the applicability of the conceptual model for understanding a range of student attitudes and orientations. For example, Collier (2000) finds that colleges can effectively promote their own version of an ideal college student identity through the development and implementation of senior year capstone courses. In a qualitative study, Grant and Breese (1997) conclude that, among African American college students, an individual's personal construction of what it means to be marginal has a greater impact on personal satisfaction than the simple state of being marginal. Research should also examine the contribution of the conceptual model for understanding students' K-12 and postsecondary educational experiences. Future research should also consider the usefulness of the conceptual model for examining other indicators of college readiness. The literature on academic tracking in high schools (see, for example, Friedkin and Thomas, 1997; Lucas and Berends, 2002; Oakes and Guiton, 1995; Spade, Columba, and Vanfossen, 1997) generally suggests that tracking and ability grouping tend to be particularly problematic for the academic preparation of socioeconomically disadvantaged students.

Finally, research that tests the proposed conceptual model should draw on the disciplinary perspectives that were the basis for this monograph (education, economics, sociology, and psychology) as well as other disciplinary and theoretical perspectives. With their attention to societal forces and structures, lenses drawn from other disciplines (such as history and political science) would likely generate new insights about the forces that promote student success and reduce differences in student success across groups (Fogg-Davis, 2004; Gelber, 2004).

Future research should also test the ways that the model may be used to develop interdisciplinary perspectives for understanding student success. Attempts to test multi- and interdisciplinary perspectives may be informed by efforts in other applied fields, including public administration. Like education, public administration draws on theoretical perspectives from other disciplines to examine problems and guide research. For example, framing the examination in terms of the contribution of educational attainment to earnings, one study in a top public administration journal shows that cognitive skills as measured in high school are related to earnings only indirectly through educational attainment (Murnane, Willett, Duhaldeborde, and Tyler, 2000). Other articles published in top journals in public administration shed light on the influence on student success of the public policy context, particularly the availability of higher education, affirmative action policies, and state financial aid policies. For example, research shows that enrollment patterns are shaped, at least in part, by the characteristics of a state's higher education system, particularly the relative numbers of two-year and four-year institutions and tuition charged by these institutions (Rouse, 1998). Other research shows that affirmative action policies affect minority and majority students differently (Mumpower, Nath, and Stewart, 2002) and that policies that consider class rather than race or ethnicity result in a smaller number of admitted students who are racial or ethnic minorities (Cancian, 1998). Based on their examination of the Georgia HOPE scholarship program, Henry and Rubenstein (2002) concluded that the availability of this merit-based state aid was associated with higher academic preparation of students during high school and a lower gap in academic achievement between African American and white high school students.

Although well positioned to adopt interdisciplinary approaches to research on student success, educational researchers must overcome at least two challenges to these approaches. First, educational researchers draw on theories and methods from a wide variety of academic disciplines, but most continue to examine student success indicators from a particular disciplinary orientation. Compared with research in other disciplines, educational research is more outcome focused than theory focused. Even in educational research, however, student success studies are still generally constrained by underlying disciplinary orientations.

A second challenge for interdisciplinary research on student success is that such research is generally less intellectually coherent than research that draws on theories and perspectives from one discipline. Conducting interdisciplinary research requires understanding the varied intellectual motivations of each discipline.

Research that successfully overcomes the challenges to interdisciplinarity will likely yield important insights into the problem of student success. This monograph shows that the knowledge base for student success consists largely of a collection of disconnected disciplinary inquiries that do not systematically canvas the range of issues and perspectives that more completely and comprehensively inform student success. Moreover, a singular disciplinary approach provides intellectual coherence at the expense of a reductionism that tends to artificially force a reality on the educational context in which success outcomes can be best understood. Only by relaxing the often unrealistic assumptions and constraints that define the coherence of the disciplines can we achieve more comprehensive and policy-relevant understandings of student success.

Conclusion

This chapter offers implications of the proposed conceptual model for policymakers, practitioners, and researchers. For policymakers and practitioners, the model underscores the importance of considering that the effects on student success of any policy or program will likely depend on various aspects of context. Policymakers and practitioners should also recognize that policies and programs do not exist in isolation but interact with both characteristics of other policies and programs as well as the characteristics of the student, family, and school context. Because multiple layers of context inform student success, no one approach will improve student success for all students. Finally, to improve our understanding of the ways that layers of context influence student success, policymakers and practitioners should support a program of research that examines various aspects of the proposed model.

The chapter also offers several recommendations for researchers. Specifically, the chapter recommends that researchers test the extent to which the proposed model may be used to bridge the research and policy or practice communities, incorporate insights from a range of methodological approaches and data sources, understand other indicators of student success, and develop multi- and interdisciplinary approaches to examining student success. The chapter concludes by stressing the critical role that educational researchers may play in both advancing multi- and interdisciplinary approaches as well as overcoming the challenges that are associated with such research.

References

Alfonso, M., Bailey, T. R., and Scott, M. (2005). The educational outcomes of occupational sub-baccalaureate students: Evidence from the 1990s. *Economics of Education Review, 24*(2), 197.

Alon, S., and Tienda, M. (2005). Assessing the "mismatch" hypothesis: Differences in college graduation rates by institutional selectivity. *Sociology of Education, 78,* 294.

Arias, O., and McMahon, W. W. (2001). Dynamic rates of return to education in the U.S. *Economics of Education Review, 20*(2), 121.

Aschaffenburg, K., and Maas, I. (1997). Cultural and educational careers: The dynamics of social reproduction. *American Sociological Review, 62*(4), 573–587.

Astin, A. H., and Oseguera, L. (2004). The declining "equity" of American higher education. *Review of Higher Education, 27,* 321–341.

Astin, A. W., Sax, L. J., and Avalos, J. (1999). Long-term effects of volunteerism during the undergraduate years. *Review of Higher Education, 22,* 187–202.

Attewell, P. (2001). The winner-take-all high school: Organizational adaptations to educational stratification. *Sociology of Education, 74*(4), 267–295.

Averett, S. L., and Burton, M. L. (1996). College attendance and the college wage premium: Differences by gender. *Economics of Education Review, 15*(1), 37.

Barling, J., Zacharatos, A., and Hepburn, C. G. (1999). Parents' job insecurity affects children's academic performance through cognitive difficulties. *Journal of Applied Psychology, 84,* 437–444.

Barron, K. E., and Harackiewicz, J. M. (2001). Achievement goals and optimal motivation: Testing multiple goal models. *Journal of Personality and Social Psychology, 80,* 706–722.

Becker, G. (1993). *Human capital* (3rd ed.). Chicago: University of Chicago Press.

Berger, M. C., and Kostal, T. (2002). Financial resources, regulation, and enrollment in U.S. public higher education. *Economics of Education Review, 21*(2), 101.

Bodvarsson, O. B., and Walker, R. L. (2004). Do parental cash transfers weaken performance in college? *Economics of Education Review, 23*(5), 483.

Borg, W. R., and Gall, M. D. (1989). *Educational research: An introduction* (5th ed.). New York: Longman.

Bourdieu, P., and Passeron, J. (1977). *Reproduction in education, society, and culture*. London: Sage.

Bowen, H. (1997). *Investment in learning: The individual and social value of American higher education* (Reprint). Baltimore: Johns Hopkins University Press.

Brackney, B. E., and Karabenick, S. A. (1995). Psychopathology and academic performance: The role of motivation and learning strategies. *Journal of Counseling Psychology, 42,* 456–465.

Bradley, K. (2000). The incorporation of women into higher education: Paradoxical outcomes? *Sociology of Education, 73*(1), 1–18.

Bridgeman, B., and Morgan, R. (1996). Success in college for students with discrepancies between performance on multiple-choice and essay tests. *Journal of Educational Psychology, 88,* 333–340.

Brown, M. C., II (2002). Good intentions: Collegiate desegregation and transdemographic enrollments. *Review of Higher Education, 25,* 263–280.

Brown, R. P., and others. (2000). Putting the "affirm" into affirmative action: Preferential selection and academic performance. *Journal of Personality and Social Psychology, 79,* 736–747.

Brown, R. P., and Josephs, R. A. (1999). A burden of proof: Stereotype relevance and gender differences in math performance. *Journal of Personality and Social Psychology, 76,* 246–257.

Burgard, D. E. (2001). Journal of the century in psychology. *The Serials Librarian, 39,* 41–56.

Cancian, M. (1998). Race-based versus class-based affirmative action in college admissions. *Journal of Policy Analysis and Management, 17,* 94–105.

Casey, M. B., Nuttall, R. L., and Pezaris, E. (1997). Mediators of gender differences in mathematics college entrance test scores: A comparison of spatial skills with internalized beliefs and anxieties. *Developmental Psychology, 33,* 669–680.

Casey, M. B., Nuttall, R., Pezaris, E., and Benbow, C. P. (1995). The influence of spatial ability on gender differences in mathematics college entrance test scores across diverse samples. *Developmental Psychology, 31,* 697–705.

Chapell, M. S., and others. (2005). Test anxiety and academic performance in undergraduate and graduate students. *Journal of Educational Psychology, 97,* 268–274.

Chavous, T. M., and others. (2003). Racial identity and academic attainment among African American adolescents. *Child Development, 74,* 1076–1090.

Chemers, M. M., Hu, L., and Garcia, B. F. (2001). Academic self-efficacy and first-year college student performance and adjustment. *Journal of Educational Psychology, 93,* 55–64.

Chen, G., Gully, S. M., Whiteman, J.-A., and Kilcullen, R. N. (2000). Examination of relationships among trait-like individual differences, state-like individual differences, and learning performance. *Journal of Applied Psychology, 85,* 835–847.

Cheng, S., and Starks, B. (2002). Racial differences in the effects of significant others on students' educational expectations. *Sociology of Education, 75*(4), 306–327.

Coleman, J. C., and others. (1964). *Equality of educational opportunity.* Washington, DC: U.S. Government Printing Office.

Collier, P. J. (2000). The effects of completing a capstone course on student identity. *Sociology of Education, 73*(4), 285–299.

Conley, D. (2001). Capital for college: Parental assets and postsecondary schooling. *Sociology of Education, 74*(1), 59–72.

Crosnoe, R. (2001). Academic orientation and parental involvement in education during high school. *Sociology of Education, 74*(3), 210–230.

Cullen, M. J., Hardison, C. M., and Sackett, P. R. (2004). Using SAT-grade and ability-job performance relationships to test predictions derived from stereotype threat theory. *Journal of Applied Psychology, 89,* 220–230.

Davies, P. G., Spencer, S. J., Quinn, D. M., and Gerhardstein, R. (2002). Consuming images: How television commercials that elicit stereotype threat can restrain women academically and professionally. *Personality and Social Psychology Bulletin, 28,* 1615–1628.

Davila, A., and Mora, M. T. (2004). The scholastic progress of students with entrepreneurial parents. *Economics of Education Review, 23*(3), 287.

Deil-Amen, R., and Rosenbaum, J. E. (2002). The unintended consequences of stigma-free remediation. *Sociology of Education, 75*(3), 249–268.

Deke, J. (2003). A study of the impact of public school spending on postsecondary educational attainment using statewide school district refinancing in Kansas. *Economics of Education Review, 22*(3), 275.

DiMaggio, P. (1982). Cultural capital and school success: The impact of status culture participation on grades of U.S. high school students. *American Sociological Review, 47*(2), 189–201.

Dumais, S. A. (2002). Cultural capital, gender, and school success: The role of habitus. *Sociology of Education, 75*(1), 44–68.

Dynarski, S. (2002). The behavioral and distributional implications of aid for college. Papers and proceedings of the one hundred fourteenth annual meeting of the American Economic Association. *American Economic Review, 92*(2), 279–285.

Ehrenberg, R. G., and Smith, C. L. (2004). Analyzing the success of student transitions from 2- to 4-year institutions within a state. *Economics of Education Review, 23*(1), 11.

Eide, E., Brewer, D. J., and Ehrenberg, R. G. (1998). Does it pay to attend an elite private college? Evidence on the effects of undergraduate college quality on graduate school attendance. *Economics of Education Review, 17*(4), 371.

Eide, E., and Waehrer, G. (1998). The role of the option value of college attendance in college major choice. *Economics of Education Review, 17*(1), 73.

Elliot, A. J., and Church, M. A. (1997). A hierarchal model of approach and avoidance achievement motivation. *Journal of Personality and Social Psychology, 72,* 218–232.

Elliot, A. J., and McGregor, H. A. (1999). Test anxiety and the hierarchical model of approach and avoidance achievement motivation. *Journal of Personality and Social Psychology, 76,* 628–644.

Elliot, A. J., McGregor, H. A., and Gable, S. (1999). Achievement goals, study strategies, and exam performance: A mediational analysis. *Journal of Educational Psychology, 91,* 549–563.

Elster, J. (1983). *Sour grapes: Studies in the subversion of rationality.* Cambridge: Cambridge University Press.

Espenshade, T. J., Hale, L. E., and Chung, C. Y. (2005). The frog pond revisited: High school academic context, class rank, and elite college admission. *Sociology of Education, 78,* 269.

Feldman, K. A., and Newcomb, T. M. (1969). *The impact of college on students.* San Francisco: Jossey-Bass.

Fleming, J. (2002). Who will succeed in college? When the SAT predicts black students' performance. *Review of Higher Education, 25,* 281–296.

Fogg-Davis, H. (2004). *Political science literature review.* New York: Social Science Research Council.

Ford, T. E., Ferguson, M. A., Brooks, J. L., and Hagadone, K. M. (2004). Coping sense of humor reduces effects of stereotype threat on women's math performance. *Personality and Social Psychology Bulletin, 30,* 643–653.

Freeman, K. (1997). Increasing African Americans' participation in higher education: African American students' perspectives. *Journal of Higher Education, 68*(5), 523–550.

Freeman, K. (1999). HBCs or PWIs? African American high school students' consideration of higher education institution types. *Review of Higher Education, 23,* 91–106.

Friedkin, N. E., and Thomas, S. L. (1997). Social positions in schooling. *Sociology of Education, 70*(4), 239–255.

Fries-Britt, S., and Turner, B. (2002). Uneven stories: Successful black collegians at a black and a white campus. *Review of Higher Education, 25,* 315–330.

Furstenberg, F. F., and others. (1999). *Managing to make it: Urban families and adolescent success.* Chicago: University of Chicago Press.

Garand, J. C., and Giles, M. W. (2003, April). Journals in the discipline: A report on a new survey of American political scientists. *PSOnline.* Retrieved June 8, 2005, from www.apsanet.org.

Gelber, S. (2004). *Transitions to college: History literature review.* New York: Social Science Research Council.

Gibbons, F. X., and others. (2000). Does social comparison make a difference? Optimism as a moderator of the relation between comparison level and academic performance. *Journal of Personality and Social Psychology, 26,* 637–648.

Gigerenzer, G., and Selton, R. (2001). *Bounded rationality.* Cambridge, MA: MIT Press.

Gintis, H. (1978). The nature of the labor exchange and the theory of capitalist production. *Review of Radical Political Economics, 8*(2), 515–531.

Glasgow, K. L., and others. (1997). Parenting styles, adolescents' attributions, and educational outcomes in nine heterogeneous high school. *Child Development, 68,* 507–529.

Gonzales, P. M., Blanton, H., and Williams, K. J. (2002). The effects of stereotype threat and double-minority status on the test performance of Latino women. *Journal of Personality and Social Psychology, 28,* 659–670.

Gonzalez, A., and Hilmer, M. J. (2006) The role of 2-year colleges in the improving situation of Hispanic postsecondary education. *Economics of Education Review, 25*(3), 249–257.

Grant, G. K., and Breese, J. R. (1997). Marginality theory and the African American student. *Sociology of Education, 70*(3), 192–205.

Grubb, W. N. (2002a). Learning and earning in the middle. Part I: National studies of pre-baccalaureate education. *Economics of Education Review, 21*(4), 299.

Grubb, W. N. (2002b). Learning and earning in the middle. Part II: State and local studies of pre-baccalaureate education. *Economics of Education Review, 21*(5), 401.

Hamrick, F. A., and Stage, F. K. (1998). High minority enrollment, high school lunch schools: Predisposition to college. *Review of Higher Education, 21*, 343–357.

Harackiewicz, J. M., Barron, K. E., Carter, S. M., and Lehto, A. T. (1997). Predictors and consequences of achievement goals in the college classroom: Maintaining interest and making the grade. *Journal of Personality and Social Psychology, 73*, 1284–1295.

Harackiewicz, J. M., and others. (2000). Short-term and long-term consequences of achievement goals: Predicting interest and performance over time. *Journal of Educational Psychology, 92*, 316–330.

Harackiewicz, J. M., Barron, K. E., Tauer, J. M., and Elliot, A. J. (2002). Predicting success in college: A longitudinal study of achievement goals and ability measures as predictors of interest and performance from freshman year through graduation. *Journal of Educational Psychology, 94*, 562–575.

Hattie, J., Biggs, J., and Purdie, N. (1996). Effects of learning skills interventions on student learning: A meta-analysis. *Review of Educational Research, 66*, 99–136.

Heller, D. E. (1997). Student price response in higher education: An update to Leslie and Brinkman. *Journal of Higher Education, 68*(6), 624–659.

Heller, D. E. (1999). The effects of tuition and state financial aid on public college enrollment. *Review of Higher Education, 23*, 65–89.

Henry, G. T., and Rubenstein, R. (2002). Paying for grades: Impact of merit-based financial aid on educational quality. *Journal of Policy Analysis and Management, 21*, 93–109.

Hill, N. E., and others. (2004). Parent academic involvement as related to school behavior, achievement, and aspirations: Demographic variations across adolescence. *Child Development, 75*, 1491–1509.

Hofferth, S. L., Boisjoly, J., and Duncan, G. J. (1998). Parents' extrafamilial resources and children's school attainment. *Sociology of Education, 71*(3), 246–268.

Hoffman, J. I., and Lowitzki, K. E. (2005). Predicting college success with high school grades and test scores: Limitations for minority students. *Review of Higher Education, 28*, 455–474.

Hong, S., and Ho, H.-Z. (2005). Direct and indirect longitudinal effects of parental involvement on student achievement: Second-order latent growth modeling across ethnic groups. *Journal of Educational Psychology, 97*, 32–42.

Hurtado, S., and Carter, D. F. (1997). Effects of college transition and perceptions of the campus racial climate on Latino college students' sense of belonging. *Sociology of Education, 70*(4), 324–345.

Ichimura, H., and Taber, C. (2002). Semiparametric reduced-form estimation of tuition subsidies. Papers and proceedings of the one hundred fourteenth annual meeting of the American Economic Association. *American Economic Review, 92*(2), 286–292.

ISI Web of Knowledge. (2003). *2003 journal citation reports, social sciences edition.* Retrieved June 13, 2005, from http://www.isiwebofknowledge.com.

Jacob, B. A. (2002). Where the boys aren't: Non-cognitive skills, returns to school, and the gender gap in higher education. *Economics of Education Review, 21*(6), 589.

Kane, T. J., and Rouse, C. E. (1995). Labor-market returns to two- and four-year college. *American Economic Review, 85*(3), 600–614.

Karen, D. (2002). Changes in access to higher education in the United States: 1980–1992. *Sociology of Education, 75*(3), 191–210.

Keane, M. P. (2002). Financial aid, borrowing constraints, and college attendance: Evidence from structural estimates. Papers and proceedings of the one hundred fourteenth annual meeting of the American Economic Association. *American Economic Review, 92*(2), 293–297.

Kerkvliet, J., and Nowell, C. (2005). Does one size fit all? University differences in the influence of wages, financial aid, and integration on student retention. *Economics of Education Review, 24*(1), 85.

Kingston, P. W. (2001). The unfulfilled promise of cultural capital theory. *Sociology of Education, 74* (Extra issue: Currents of thought: Sociology of education at the dawn of the 21st century), 88–99.

Kirk, J., and Miller, M. L. (1986). Reliability and validity in qualitative research. *Qualitative Research Methods Series* (Vol. 1). Newbury Park, CA: Sage.

Kirst, M. W., and Venezia, A. (Eds.). (2004). *From high school to college: Improving opportunities for success in postsecondary education.* San Francisco: Jossey-Bass.

Kmett, C. M., Arkes, H. R., and Jones, S. K. (1999). The influence of decision aids on high school students' satisfaction with their college choice decision. *Journal of Personality and Social Psychology, 25,* 1293–1301.

Lamont, M., and Lareau, A. (1988). Cultural capital: Allusions, gaps, and glissandos in recent theoretical developments. *Sociological Theory, 6,* 153–168.

Larose, S., and Roy, R. (1995). Test of reactions and adaptation in college (TRAC): A new measure of learning propensity for college students. *Journal of Educational Psychology, 87,* 293–306.

Leigh, D. E., and Gill, A. M. (2003). Do community colleges really divert students from earning bachelor's degrees? *Economics of Education Review, 22*(1), 23.

Leigh, D. E., and Gill, A. M. (2004). The effect of community colleges on changing students' educational aspirations. *Economics of Education Review, 23*(1), 95.

Leontaridi, M. R. (1998). Segmented labour markets: Theory and evidence. *Journal of Economic Surveys, 12*(1), 63–101.

Lucas, S. R., and Berends, M. (2002). Sociodemographic diversity, correlated achievement, and de facto tracking. *Sociology of Education, 75*(4), 328–348.

Lumley, M. A., and Provenzano, K. M. (2003). Stress management through written emotional disclosure improves academic performance among college students with physical symptoms. *Journal of Educational Psychology, 95,* 641–649.

Mael, F. A. (1998). Single-sex and coeducational schooling: Relationships to socioemotional and academic development. *Review of Educational Research, 68,* 101–129.

Mahoney, J. L., Cairns, B. D., and Farmer, T. W. (2003). Promoting interpersonal competence and educational success through extracurricular activity participation. *Journal of Educational Psychology, 95,* 409–418.

Manski, C. F. (1993). Dynamic choice in social settings. *Journal of Econometrics, 58,* 121–136.

March, J. G. (1994). *A primer on decision making. How decisions happen.* New York: Free Press.

Marx, D. M., and Roman, J. S. (2002). Female role models: Protecting women's math test performance. *Journal of Personality and Social Psychology, 28,* 1183–1193.

Marx, K. (1891). Wage Labor and Capital. Trans. F. Engels. Available online at http://www.marxists.org/archive/marx/works/1847/wage-labour/index.htm.

McDonough, P. M. (1997). *Choosing colleges: How social class and schools structure opportunity.* Albany: State University of New York Press.

Mendoza-Denton, R., and others. (2002). Sensitivity to status-based rejection: Implications for African American students' college experience. *Journal of Personality and Social Psychology, 83,* 896–918.

Mincer, J. (1974). *Schooling, experience, and earnings.* New York: National Bureau of Economic Research.

Minicozzi, A. (2005). The short term effect of educational debt on job decisions. *Economics of Education Review, 24*(4), 417.

Monks, J. (1997). The impact of college timing on earnings. *Economics of Education Review, 16*(4), 419.

Monks, J. (2001). Loan burdens and educational outcomes. *Economics of Education Review, 20*(6), 545.

Muller, C., and Schiller, K. S. (2000). Leveling the playing field? Students' educational attainment and states' performance testing. *Sociology of Education, 73*(3), 196–218.

Mumpower, J. L., Nath, R., and Stewart, T. R. (2002). Affirmative action, duality of error, and the consequences of mispredicting the academic performance of African American college applicants. *Journal of Policy Analysis and Management, 21,* 63–77.

Murnane, R. J., Willett, J. B., Duhaldeborde, Y., and Tyler, J. H. (2000). How important are the cognitive skills of teenagers in predicting subsequent earnings? *Journal of Policy Analysis and Management, 19,* 547–568.

Nagda, B. A., and others. (1998). Undergraduate student-faculty research partnerships affect student retention. *Review of Higher Education, 22,* 55–72.

National Center for Education Statistics. (2004). *Digest of education statistics, 2004.* Washington, DC: National Center for Education Statistics.

National Center for Public Policy and Higher Education. (2006). *Measuring up, 2006.* San Jose, CA: National Center for Public Policy and Higher Education.

Niu, S. X., Tienda, M., and Cortes, K. (2006). College selectivity and the Texas top 10% law. *Economics of Education Review, 25*(3), 259–272.

Oakes, J., and Guiton, G. (1995). Matchmaking: The dynamics of high school tracking decisions. *American Educational Research Journal, 32*(1), 3–33.

O'Brien, L. T., and Crandall, C. S. (2003). Stereotype threat and arousal: Effects on women's math performance. *Personality and Social Psychology Bulletin, 29,* 782–789.

O'Brien, N. P. (2001). Journals of the century in education. *The Serials Librarian, 39,* 95–102.

Oswald, F. L., and others. (2004). Developing a biodata measure and situational judgment inventory as predictors of college student performance. *Journal of Applied Psychology, 89,* 187–207.

Pajares, F. (1996). Self-efficacy beliefs in academic settings. *Review of Educational Research, 66,* 543–578.

Pascarella, E. T., and Terenzini, P. T. (1993). *How college affects students.* San Francisco: Jossey-Bass.

Pascarella, E. T., and Terenzini, P. T. (2005). *How college affects students: A third decade of research* (Vol. 2). San Francisco: Jossey-Bass.

Pascarella, E. T., Wolniak, G. C., Flowers, L. A., and Pierson, C. T. (2004). The role of race in the development of plans for a graduate degree. *Review of Higher Education, 27,* 299–320.

Passeron, J., and Bourdieu, P. (1973). Cultural reproduction and social reproduction. In R. Brown (Ed.), *Knowledge, education, and social change.* London: Tavistock.

Paulsen, M. B., and St. John, E. P. (2002). Social class and college costs: Examining the financial nexus between college choice and persistence. *Journal of Higher Education, 73*(2), 189–236.

Perna, L. W. (2000). Differences in the decision to enroll in college among African Americans, Hispanics, and whites. *Journal of Higher Education, 71,* 117–141.

Perna, L. W. (2004). Understanding the decision to enroll in graduate school: Sex and racial/ethnic group differences. *Journal of Higher Education, 75,* 487–527.

Perna, L. W. (2006a). Studying college choice: A proposed conceptual model. In J. C. Smart (Ed.), *Higher education: Handbook of theory and research, Volume XXI* (pp. 99–157). Dordrecht, The Netherlands: Springer.

Perna, L. W. (2006b). Understanding the relationship between information about college costs and financial aid and students' college-related behaviors. *American Behavioral Scientist, 49,* 1620–1635.

Perna, L. W. (in press). Paying college prices: Understanding high school students' perceptions of loans. *Research in Higher Education.*

Perna, L. W., Steele, P., Woda, S., and Hibbert, T. (2005). State public policies and the racial/ethnic stratification of college access and choice in the state of Maryland. *Review of Higher Education, 28,* 245–272.

Perna, L. W., and Titus, M. (2004). Understanding differences in the choice of college attended: The role of state public policies. *Review of Higher Education, 27,* 501–525.

Perna, L. W., and Titus, M. (2005). The relationship between parental involvement as social capital and college enrollment: An examination of racial/ethnic group differences. *Journal of Higher Education, 76,* 485–518.

Perry, R. P., Hladkyj, S., Pekrun, R. H., and Pelletier, S. T. (2001). Academic control and action control in the achievement of college students: A longitudinal field study. *Journal of Educational Psychology, 93,* 776–789.

Plank, S. B., and Jordan, W. J. (2001). Effects of information, guidance, and actions on post-secondary destinations: A study of talent loss. *American Educational Research Journal, 38*(4), 947.

Quinn, D. M., Kahng, S. K., and Crocker, J. (2004). Discreditable: Stigma effects of revealing a mental illness history on test performance. *Personality and Social Psychology Bulletin, 30,* 803–815.

Ramirez, F. O., and Wotipka, C. M. (2001). Slowly but surely? The global expansion of women's participation in science and engineering fields of study, 1972–92. *Sociology of Education, 74*(3), 231–251.

Rau, W., and Durand, A. (2000). The academic ethic and college grades: Does hard work help students to "make the grade"? *Sociology of Education, 73*(1), 19–38.

Regina, D.-A., and James, E. R. (2004). Charter building and labor market contacts in two-year colleges. *Sociology of Education, 77,* 245.

Robins, R. W., and Beer, J. S. (2001). Positive illusions about the self: Short-term benefits and long-term costs. *Journal of Personality and Social Psychology,* 80, 340–352.

Roksa, J. (2005). Double disadvantage or blessing in disguise? Understanding the relationship between college major and employment sector. *Sociology of Education, 78*(3), 207.

Rouse, C. E. (1998). Do two-year colleges increase overall educational attainment? Evidence from the states. *Journal of Policy Analysis and Management, 17,* 595–620.

Ruban, L. M., and McCoach, D. B. (2005). Gender differences in explaining grades using structural equation modeling. *Review of Higher Education, 28,* 475–502.

St. John, E. P., and Asker, E. H. (2001). The role of finances in student choice: A review of theory and research. In M. B. Paulsen, and J. C. Smart (Eds.), *The finance of higher education: Theory, research, policy, and practice* (pp. 419–438). New York: Agathon Press.

St. John, E. P., and Paulsen, M. B. (2001). The finance of higher education: Implications for theory, research, policy and practice. In M. B. Paulsen and J. C. Smart (Eds.), *The finance of higher education: Theory, research, policy, and practice* (pp. 545–568). New York: Agathon Press.

St. John, E. P., Paulsen, M. B., and Carter, D. F. (2005). Diversity, college costs, and postsecondary opportunity: An examination of the financial nexus between college choice and persistence. *Journal of Higher Education, 76,* 545–569.

Sandy, J., Gonzalez, A., and Hilmer, M. J. (2006). Alternative paths to college completion: Effect of attending a 2-year school on the probability of completing a 4-year degree. *Economics of Education Review, 25,* 463–471.

Schleef, D. (2000). "That's a good question!" Exploring motivations for law and business school choice. *Sociology of Education, 73*(3), 155–174.

Shilkret, R., and Nigrosh, E. E. (1997). Assessing students' plans for college. *Journal of Counseling Psychology, 44,* 222–231.

Siegfried, J., and Getz, M. (2006). Where do the children of professors attend college? *Economics of Education Review, 26,* 201–210.

Simon, H. (1957). *Models of man. Social and rational: Mathematical essays on rational human behavior in a society setting.* New York: Wiley.

Singell, J. L. D. (2004). Come and stay a while: Does financial aid effect retention conditioned on enrollment at a large public university? *Economics of Education Review, 23*(5), 459.

Sireci, S. G., Zanetti, M., and Berger, J. B. (2003). Recent and anticipated changes in postsecondary admissions: A survey of New England colleges and universities. *Review of Higher Education, 26,* 323–342.

Snyder, C. R., and others. (2002). Hope and academic success in college. *Journal of Educational Psychology, 94,* 820–826.

Social Science Research Council. (2005). *Questions that matter: Setting the research agenda on access and success in postsecondary education.* New York: Social Science Research Council.

Spade, J. Z., Columba, L., and Vanfossen, B. E. (1997). Tracking in mathematics and science: Courses and course-selection procedures. *Sociology of Education, 70*(2), 108–127.

Springer, L., Stanne, M. E., and Donovan, S. S. (1999). Effects of small-group learning on undergraduates in science, mathematics, engineering, and technology: A meta-analysis. *Review of Educational Research, 69,* 21–51.

Stage, F. K., and Kloosterman, P. (1995). Gender, beliefs, and achievement in remedial college-level mathematics. *Journal of Higher Education, 66*(3), 294–311.

Stapleton, L., and Thomas, S. L. (2008). Sources and issues in the use of national datasets for pedagogy and research. In A. O'Connell and B. McCoach (Eds.). *Multilevel modeling of educational data.* Charlotte, NC: Information Age Publishing.

Steele, C. M., and Aronson, J. (1995). Stereotype threat and the intellectual test performance of African Americans. *Journal of Personality and Social Psychology, 69,* 797–811.

Strage, A., and Brandt, T. S. (1999). Authoritative parenting and college students' academic adjustment and success. *Journal of Educational Psychology, 91,* 146–156.

Stumpf, H., and Stanley, J. C. (1996). Gender-related differences on the College Board's Advanced Placement and Achievement Tests, 1982–1992. *Journal of Educational Psychology, 88,* 353–364.

Surette, B. J. (2001). Transfer from two-year to four-year college: An analysis of gender differences. *Economics of Education Review, 20*(2), 151.

Svanum, S., and Zody, Z. B. (2001). Psychopathology and college grades. *Journal of Counseling Psychology, 48,* 72–76.

Teranishi, R. T., and others. (2004). The choice-choice process for Asian Pacific Americans: Ethnicity and socioeconomic class in context. *Review of Higher Education, 29,* 527–551.

Thomas, S. L. (2000). Ties that bind: A social network approach to understanding student integration and persistence. *Journal of Higher Education, 71*(5), 571–615.

Thomas, S. L., and Heck, R. H. (2001). Analysis of large-scale secondary data in higher education: Potential perils associated with complex sample designs. *Research in Higher Education, 42*(5), 517–540.

Thomas, S. L., and Perna, L. W. (2004). The opportunity agenda: A reexamination of post-secondary reward and opportunity. In J. C. Smart (Ed.), *Higher education: Handbook of theory and research* (Vol. 19, pp. 43–84). Dordrecht, The Netherlands: Kluwer Academic Publishers.

Thomas, S. L., and Zhang, L. (2005). Changing rates of return to college quality and academic major in the United States: Who gets good jobs in America? *Research in Higher Education, 46*(4), 437–459.

Tierney, W. G., and Jun, A. (2001). A university helps prepare low-income youths for college: Tracking school success. Special issue: The social role of higher education. *Journal of Higher Education, 72*(2), 205–225.

Topping, K. (1998). Peer assessment between students in colleges and universities. *Review of Educational Research, 68,* 249–276.

Toutkoushian, R. K. (2001). Do parental income and educational attainment affect the initial choices of New Hampshire's college-bound students? *Economics of Education Review, 20*(3), 245.

Toutkoushian, R. K., and Smart, J. C. (2001). Do institutional characteristics affect student gains from college? *Review of Higher Education, 25,* 39–61.

Tseng, V. (2004). Family interdependence and academic adjustment to college: Youth from immigrant and U.S.-born families. *Child Development, 75,* 966–983.

U.S. Census Bureau. (2004). Table PINC–03. Educational attainment–People 25 years old and over, by total money earnings in 2001, work experience in 2001, age, race, Hispanic origin, and sex. Retrieved March 2, 2006, from http://ferret.bls.census.gov/macro/032002/perinc/new03_000.htm.

VandeWalle, D., Cron, W. L., and Slocum, J. W. Jr. (2001). The role of goal orientation following performance feedback. *Journal of Applied Psychology, 86*(4): 629–640.

Ver Ploeg, M. (2002). Children from disrupted families as adults: Family structure, college attendance, and college completion. *Economics of Education Review, 21*(2), 171.

Villanova, P. (1996). Predictive validity of situational constraints in general versus specific performance domains. *Journal of Applied Psychology, 81,* 532–547.

Walpole, M. (2003). Socioeconomic status and college: How SES affects college experiences and outcomes. *Review of Higher Education, 27,* 45–73.

Western Interstate Commission on Higher Education. (2005). *Knocking at the college door.* Boulder, CO: Western Interstate Commission on Higher Education.

Western Interstate Commission on Higher Education. (2008). *Knocking at the college door: Projections of high school graduates by state and race/ethnicity, 1992–2022.* Boulder, CO: Western Interstate Commission on Higher Education.

Wilson, S. B., Mason, T. W., and Ewing, M. J. (1997). Evaluating the impact of receiving university-based counseling services on student retention. *Journal of Counseling Psychology, 44,* 316–320.

Wolters, C. A. (1998). Self-regulated learning and college students' regulation of motivation. *Journal of Educational Psychology, 90,* 224–235.

Wong, M. M. (2000). The relations among causality orientations, academic experience, academic performance, and academic commitment. *Journal of Personality and Social Psychology, 26,* 315–326.

Zhang, L. (2005a). Advance to graduate education: The effect of college quality and undergraduate major. *Review of Higher Education, 28,* 313–338.

Zhang, L. (2005b). Do measures of college quality matter? The effect of college quality on graduates' earnings. *Review of Higher Education, 28,* 571–596.

Name Index

Subject Index

A

Academic performance
  gender differences in, 38–39
  race/ethnicity differences in, 38
  single-sex institution impact on, 49
  student identity related to, 47–48.
    See also Student success; Students
African Americans
  academic performance gaps between
    whites and, 38
  undergraduate student research
    opportunities for, 50. *See also* Racial/
    ethnicity differences
American Educational Research Journal,
  9, 19
American Indian students, 58

B

Beginning Postsecondary Student Survey,
  25

C

College enrollment
  impact of financial aid programs on,
    57–58
  models incorporating economic theories
    on, 31–32
  studies on African American rates of, 38
Conceptual model. *See* Student success
  conceptual model
Context
  disciplinary family, 40–44

disciplinary internal, 35–40
disciplinary school, 44–50
disciplinary social, economic, and policy,
  50–53
as financial aid program component, 56
situated, 32–33. *See also* Student
  success
Cooperative Institutional Research
  Program, 25
*Cultural Reproduction and Social
  Reproduction* (Passeron and Bourdieu),
  16
Current Population Survey, 25

D

Disciplinary approaches
  economics, 13*e*, 14–15
  education, 13*e*, 17–19
  methodologies used student success
    research, 24*e*
  psychology, 12*e*, 17
  six conclusions about, 11
  sociology, 12*e*–13*e*, 15–16. *See also*
    Journals; Student success conceptual
    model

E

ECMC Group Foundation, 58
Economics
  family context of student success in,
    40–41
  internal context of student success in, 36

success outcomes examined in articles of, 22e–23e
theoretical perspectives on student success in various disciplines, 12e–13e
top ones by discipline (2003), 8e
variations across disciplines in unit of analysis, 26
variations in aspects of student success examined, 19–21
variations in attention to differences across groups, 27–29
variations in attention to student success by, 19
variations in methodological approaches/sources of data, 21–26. See also Disciplinary approaches; Research

K

K-12 education
  public financing of, 51
  research for understanding experience of, 61
  student success tied to experiences of, 46–48, 52. See also Education

L

Layer One: internal context
  description of, 35
  economics, 36
  education, 39
  psychology, 36–39
  sociology, 36
Layer Two: family context
  description of, 40
  economics, 40–41
  education, 43–44
  psychology, 42–43
  sociology, 41–42
Layer Three: school context
  description of, 44
  economics, 44–46
  education, 49–50
  psychology, 48–49
  sociology, 46–48

Layer Four: social, economic, policy context
  description of, 50–51
  economics, 51
  education, 52
  psychology, 52
  sociology, 51–52

M

"Multiple goals" perspective, 37

N

National Center for Education Statistics, 1
National Center for Public Policy and Higher Education, 6
National Educational Longitudinal Survey (1988), 18, 25
National Longitudinal Study of Youth, 25
National Study of Student Learning, 25

P

Panel Study of Income Dynamics, 25
Pell grant program, 1
Policy recommendations
  on future research to help development policy, 59–60
  for using multiple methods and theoretical perspectives, 58
  proposed conceptual model implications for, 55–58
  to recognize interaction between policy/programs, 56–57
  to recognize multiple layers of context, 56
  to recognize that program variation reduces gaps, 57–58
Proposed conceptual model. See Student success conceptual model
Psychological disorders, 38
Psychology
  family context of student success in, 42–43
  internal context of student success in, 36–39
  school context of student success in, 48–49

Layer Two: family context by discipline of, 40–44
Layer Three: school context by discipline of, 44–50
Layer Four: social, economic, and policy context by discipline of, 50–53
overview of proposed, 29–34
procedures for proposed, 7–10
SSRC's approach to developing, 4–5. *See also* Disciplinary approaches
Student success gaps
examining existing, 1; three barriers to identifying, 2–3
Students
identity development by, 47–48
situated context of, 32–33. *See also* Academic performance

Subbaccaluareate labor market, 45

T
Test taking skills, 48–49
TRIO programs, 1

U
UCLA's Higher Education Research Initiative, 25
U.S. Census Bureau, 45
U.S. Department of Education, 25

W
Western Interstate Commission on Higher Education (2005, 2008), 2

About the Authors

Laura W. Perna is an associate professor in the Higher Education Management program in the Graduate School of Education at the University of Pennsylvania. Her scholarship uses an integrated theoretical approach and a variety of analytical techniques to understand the ways that individual characteristics, social structures, and public policies separately and together enable and restrict the ability of women, racial or ethnic minorities, and individuals of lower socioeconomic status to obtain the economic, social, and political opportunities associated with two aspects of higher education: access as a student and employment as a faculty member.

Scott L. Thomas is professor of education at the Claremont Graduate University's School of Educational Studies. His work focuses on stratification in higher education, with a special interest in issues relating to college access and the secondary school achievement gap. Thomas also has a line of methodological work that focuses on multilevel models and social network analysis. His work in this area includes a book, *An Introduction to Multilevel Modeling Techniques* (with Ron Heck, published by Lawrence Erlbaum and Associates) and related articles in a variety of refereed journals.

About the ASHE Higher Education Report Series

Since 1983, the ASHE (formerly ASHE-ERIC) Higher Education Report Series has been providing researchers, scholars, and practitioners with timely and substantive information on the critical issues facing higher education. Each monograph presents a definitive analysis of a higher education problem or issue, based on a thorough synthesis of significant literature and institutional experiences. Topics range from planning to diversity and multiculturalism, to performance indicators, to curricular innovations. The mission of the Series is to link the best of higher education research and practice to inform decision making and policy. The reports connect conventional wisdom with research and are designed to help busy individuals keep up with the higher education literature. Authors are scholars and practitioners in the academic community. Each report includes an executive summary, review of the pertinent literature, descriptions of effective educational practices, and a summary of key issues to keep in mind to improve educational policies and practice.

The Series is one of the most peer reviewed in higher education. A National Advisory Board made up of ASHE members reviews proposals. A National Review Board of ASHE scholars and practitioners reviews completed manuscripts. Six monographs are published each year and they are approximately 120 pages in length. The reports are widely disseminated through Jossey-Bass and John Wiley & Sons, and they are available online to subscribing institutions through Wiley InterScience (http://www.interscience.wiley.com).

Call for Proposals

The ASHE Higher Education Report Series is actively looking for proposals. We encourage you to contact one of the editors, Dr. Kelly Ward (kaward@wsu.edu) or Dr. Lisa Wolf-Wendel (lwolf@ku.edu), with your ideas.

Theoretical Perspectives on Student Success

Recent Titles

ASHE HIGHER EDUCATION REPORT
Order Form
SUBSCRIPTIONS AND SINGLE ISSUES

DISCOUNTED BACK ISSUES:

Use this form to receive **20% off** all back issues of ASHE Higher Education Report. All single issues priced at **$22.40** (normally $28.00)

TITLE	ISSUE NO.	ISBN
_____	_____	_____
_____	_____	_____
_____	_____	_____

Call 888-378-2537 or see mailing instructions below. When calling, mention the promotional code, JB7ND, to receive your discount.

SUBSCRIPTIONS: _(1 year, 6 issues)_

☐ New Order   ☐ Renewal

U.S.	☐ Individual: $165	☐ Institutional: $199
Canada/Mexico	☐ Individual: $165	☐ Institutional: $235
All Others	☐ Individual: $201	☐ Institutional: $310

Call 888-378-2537 or see mailing and pricing instructions below. Online subscriptions are available at www.interscience.wiley.com.

Copy or detach page and send to:
John Wiley & Sons, Journals Dept., 5th Floor
989 Market Street, San Francisco, CA 94103-1741

Order Form can also be faxed to: 888-481-2665

	SHIPPING CHARGES:		
Issue/Subscription Amount: $ _____			
Shipping Amount: $ _____	SURFACE	Domestic	Canadian
(for single issues only—subscription prices include shipping)	First Item	$5.00	$6.00
Total Amount: $ _____	Each Add'l Item	$3.00	$1.50

(No sales tax for U.S. subscriptions. Canadian residents, add GST for subscription orders. Individual rate subscriptions must be paid by personal check or credit card. Individual rate subscriptions may not be resold as library copies.)

☐ Payment enclosed (U.S. check or money order only. All payments must be in U.S. dollars.)

☐ VISA ☐ MC ☐ Amex # _____ Exp. Date _____

Card Holder Name _____ Card Issue # _____

Signature _____ Day Phone _____

☐ Bill Me (U.S. institutional orders only. Purchase order required.)

Purchase order # _____
Federal Tax ID13559302   GST 89102 8052

Name _____

Address _____

Phone _____ E-mail _____

JB7ND

ASHE-ERIC HIGHER EDUCATION REPORT IS NOW AVAILABLE ONLINE AT WILEY INTERSCIENCE

What is Wiley InterScience?

Wiley InterScience is the dynamic online content service from John Wiley & Sons delivering the full text of over 300 leading scientific, technical, medical, and professional journals, plus major reference works, the acclaimed Current Protocols laboratory manuals, and even the full text of select Wiley print books online.

What are some special features of Wiley InterScience?

Wiley Interscience Alerts is a service that delivers table of contents via e-mail for any journal available on Wiley InterScience as soon as a new issue is published online.

Early View is Wiley's exclusive service presenting individual articles online as soon as they are ready, even before the release of the compiled print issue. These articles are complete, peer-reviewed, and citable.

CrossRef is the innovative multi-publisher reference linking system enabling readers to move seamlessly from a reference in a journal article to the cited publication, typically located on a different server and published by a different publisher.

How can I access Wiley InterScience?

Visit http://www.interscience.wiley.com.

Guest Users can browse Wiley InterScience for unrestricted access to journal Tables of Contents and Article Abstracts, or use the powerful search engine. *Registered Users* are provided with a *Personal Home Page* to store and manage customized alerts, searches, and links to favorite journals and articles. Additionally, Registered Users can view free Online Sample Issues and preview selected material from major reference works. *Licensed Customers* are entitled to access full-text journal articles in PDF, with select journals also offering full-text HTML.

How do I become an Authorized User?

Authorized Users are individuals authorized by a paying Customer to have access to the journals in Wiley InterScience. For example, a University that subscribes to Wiley journals is considered to be the Customer.

Faculty, staff and students authorized by the University to have access to those journals in Wiley InterScience are Authorized Users. Users should contact their Library for information on which Wiley journals they have access to in Wiley InterScience.

ASK YOUR INSTITUTION ABOUT WILEY INTERSCIENCE TODAY!